T0021510

ALSO BY KELLEY KEEHN

Talk Money to Me

Protecting You and Your Money

A Canadian's Guide to Money-Smart Living

The Money Book for Everyone Else

She Inc.

The Prosperity Factor for Kids

The Woman's Guide to Money

The Prosperity Factor for Women

RICH GIRL, BROKE GIRL

SAVE BETTER, INVEST SMARTER, AND EARN FINANCIAL FREEDOM

KELLEY KEEHN

Published by Simon & Schuster

New York London Toronto Sydney New Delhi

Simon & Schuster Canada
A Division of Simon & Schuster, Inc.
166 King Street East, Suite 300
Toronto, Ontario M5A 1J3

This publication contains the opinions and ideas of its author. It is sold with the understanding that neither the author nor the publisher is engaged in rendering legal, tax, investment, insurance, financial, accounting, or other professional advice or services. If the reader requires such advice or services, a competent professional should be consulted. Relevant laws vary from province to province. The strategies outlined in this book may not be suitable for every individual, and are not guaranteed or warranted to produce any particular results.

No warranty is made with respect to the accuracy or completeness of the information contained herein, and both the author and the publisher specifically disclaim any responsibility for any liability, loss or risk, personal or otherwise, which is incurred as a consequence, directly or indirectly, of the use and application of any of the contents of this book.

The consumer proposal cost chart has been reprinted with the permission of Hoyes, Michalos & Associates Inc. Licensed Insolvency Trustees. The City Car graphics have been reprinted with permission of Envato and were created by vintagio. The Finance & Economy Infographic for PowerPoint graphics have been reprinted with permission of Envato.

The investment calculations were determined by using Calculator.net's financial investment calculator. The credit card payment calculations were determined by using Bankrate.com's credit card payoff calculator. The line of credit payment calculations were determined by using TD.com's personal loan and line of credit payment calculator.

This Simon & Schuster Canada edition December 2021

SIMON & SCHUSTER CANADA and colophon are trademarks of Simon & Schuster, Inc.

For information about special discounts for bulk purchases, please contact Simon & Schuster Special Sales at 1-800-268-3216 or CustomerService@simonandschuster.ca.

Manufactured in the United States of America

Interior book design by Joy O'Meara

10 9 8 7 6 5 4 3 2 1

Library and Archives Canada Cataloguing in Publication

Title: Rich girl, broke girl : save better, invest smarter, and earn financial freedom / Kelley Keehn.
Names: Keehn, Kelley, 1975– author.
Identifiers: Canadiana (print) 20210215976 | Canadiana (ebook) 20210216034 | ISBN 9781982160517 (softcover) | ISBN 9781982160524 (ebook)
Subjects: LCSH: Women—Finance, Personal.
Classification: LCC HG179 .K4284 2021 | DDC 332.0240082—dc23

ISBN 978-1-9821-6051-7
ISBN 978-1-9821-6052-4 (ebook)

To Kathy and Wyatt

Author's Note

While all of the stories and anecdotes described herein are based on true experiences, the names, situations, and some details have been altered to protect individual privacy. Neither the author nor the publisher is engaged in rendering legal, accounting, financial, or other professional services by publishing this book. As a precaution, each individual situation should be addressed with an appropriate professional to ensure adequate evaluation and planning are applied. The author and publisher specifically disclaim any liability, loss, or risk that may be incurred as a consequence, directly or indirectly, of the use and application of any of the contents of this work. The material in this book is intended as a general source of information only and should not be construed as offering specific tax, legal, financial, or investment advice. Every effort has been made to ensure that the material is correct at the time of publication.

Interest rates, market conditions, tax rulings, and other investment factors are subject to rapid change. Individuals should consult with their personal tax advisor, Chartered Professional Accountant, Certified Financial Planner, Chartered Financial Analyst, or legal professional before taking any action based upon the information contained in this book.

Contents

RICH GIRL, BROKE GIRL

Introduction

Were you ever told that, as a woman, you could financially achieve anything, dream as big as any man, accomplish anything you set your mind to? And when you tried and didn't succeed right out of the gate, what happened then? If you're anything like me (and countless other women), you were warned not to mess up again. You might have even been blamed for trying. Maybe you were told that money isn't your strong suit and that you should probably leave finances to someone else in your life. Perhaps people laughed and told you to "marry rich," to count on others not only to bring in the purse but to control the strings for you, too.

Been there, heard that before. Many women have. And that's not to say that women haven't come far. Just think of your grandmother or great-grandmother. Could she vote? Could she own property? Did she have her own bank account?

We have come a long way, and that's true in a financial sense, too. Today, women are more powerful and wealthy than ever before. Women hold 40 percent of global wealth.[1] In Canada, women control one-third of the country's financial assets. By 2028, Canadian women will control $3.8 trillion.[2] American women already control 51 percent of their nation's wealth—an estimated $14 trillion.[3] That number is expected to increase to nearly $22 trillion over the next forty years.

Ladies: that triumphant news is worth a tip of the hat. But we still have so far to go. Believe it or not, younger generations are taking less charge of their finances than previous ones—even when the ladies are the primary breadwinners in their households! Fifty-six percent of women defer to a spouse on investments. Eighty-five percent of women who defer financial decisions to their husbands believe their spouses know more about money matters than they do.[4] Often, this is grossly untrue!

Fear holds us back, and ignorance, too. Here's the hard truth: you're not truly free in life until you achieve *financial equality and financial literacy*. Even if you rely on a spouse for support, it doesn't mean you can't or shouldn't understand finances and your money situation. Oh, and like I said before, young ladies, I'm looking at you. Why? Because 61 percent of millennial women are deferring to a spouse on financial matters.[5]

Old misconceptions and traditions die hard. I've heard the excuses from women of every generation:

"I'm not good with money."

"I don't get math."

"I don't have time."

"What's the point?"

Money is like oxygen. We all need it to live and to breathe easy. Would you let someone else control its supply? Deferring financial power has taken both a financial and a psychological toll on women. The proof:

- Two-thirds of women whose partners are the primary breadwinners feel trapped.
- Seven in ten women wish they had more power in their financial futures.
- 64 percent of women wish they had their own money set aside just in case.[6]

What does all of this tell us? Women often feel paralyzed when it comes to money management. We dread it. And because we dread it, we let others handle it. And sometimes, that's not to our benefit. It also bears mentioning that women tend to hate negotiating when it involves money, especially when it comes to their salaries. This means we're losing money that we've worked hard for, and we risk falling behind our male peers.

There must be a better way, right? The good news: there is. And I'm here to help. But first, let me tell you a bit about myself. My mom and dad split when I was eight years old, and my mom raised me and my two brothers on her own. Without any education or experience, she was thrust into the workforce to care for her family by herself. The only job she could find that allowed her to be home for us after school was as a waitress.

She worked hard to make sure we had food on the table. She was always incredibly frugal, but even she knew the value of a little splurge now and again. She loved flowers. She always said they brightened a room and filled it with richness. If there were flowers on our table, everything was okay. Each paycheque my mom received, she set aside a dollar for a few fresh carnations. I can see them even now, a few strong blooms in an old ceramic vase.

Those flowers kept my mother going; they inspired her and offered hope for the future. They connected her with a sense of plenty and possibility even when we had so little. Now when people ask me how they're supposed to get through, how they can dig themselves out of financial holes when they feel hopeless and powerless, I tell them about my mother and her carnations. On a path from financial struggle to financial freedom, look for the small things that keep you going. Remember to see the flower, the brightness in the room, because that's what will motivate you to carry on.

When it comes to money, there's a sinister myth that one day your finances will simply be magically fixed. Please hear me when I say that this thinking needs to be disrupted. My mother's life eventually got a bit easier, but it took years and years of working and learning for her to gradually find her financial footing. Remember this: what we appreciate appreciates. If you appreciate your earnings, they'll likely go up. If you value each dollar you make, you probably will save some—and earn interest!

Let me share something an acquaintance said to me a while back. I told him I'd been feeling great since working with a personal trainer for the last couple of years. "Wonderful! Now you can check that off your to-do list," he said.

I was confused. Did he really believe I should simply stop exercising just because I was feeling good? But then I thought of how people think about money, and instantly I could see the parallel. So many of us think we can fix our credit score or wipe out one debt, and then everything will be fine. But true and lasting financial security is more like exercising or eating right—it's something you commit to as a habit, and when you do, you'll reap the rewards over the long term. Don't just save once and then ignore your investments. Don't clear out that debt just to overspend the next time. Just as with your health, financial fitness is a long-term commitment.

Let me tell you something about "rich girls." Rich girls know that a steady focus on finance pays the best returns. Rich girls know that spending and saving have to be balanced. Rich girls know you can't live a good life if you're staying awake all night worrying about money.

Maybe you're thinking, "This isn't for me. I don't even want to be a rich girl." Well, let's talk about that. "Rich" doesn't mean spending every moment of your day chasing money, power, and fame. It doesn't mean having millions of dollars in the bank, either. Everyone has different goals. If you're proud that you were thousands of dollars in debt and you changed your financial circumstances by becoming debt-free decades sooner than you thought, or if you feel good about yourself because you saved hard for an emergency fund by investing a little bit every month, guess what? You're a richer girl than you were before in two important ways—richer in dollars and in confidence. Let's have a look at some of the differences between rich girls and broke girls.

Rich Girls	*Broke Girls*
Know little things add up over time.	Spend until there's nothing left.
Prime themselves with positive self-talk and invest in their financial literacy.	Get frustrated easily and hand off financial decisions to others.
Pay attention to fees, charges, and debt interest.	Rarely open bank or credit card statements.
Know how to negotiate financial matters.	Complain about not having enough money but avoid money talk.

Rich Girls	*Broke Girls*
Research major spending decisions like buying a car, or renting or owning a home.	Indulge in retail therapy when they're upset or to keep up with peers.
Consult financial professionals for help.	Don't know what a financial planner does.
Talk money with friends and colleagues.	Hide their money troubles and never ask for help.
Automate savings monthly, no matter how small or large.	Never save. When money is put aside, there is always a spree that gobbles it up.
Never gamble. Have investments that are calculated and shrewd.	Want to win money rather than earn it and are always looking to "marry rich" or find a scheme to end all their money woes.

In the chapters that follow, you'll learn financial lessons through case studies of various women (none are real, but I hope they seem familiar). These composite women represent all of us. You'll meet the woman who innocently let her loafer girlfriend move into her home a few years ago and didn't realize she is now entitled to a large chunk of it, the wife who never paid attention to her finances until after her bankruptcy, and the entrepreneurial dreamer who needed a major wake-up call to make her financial fantasies a reality.

It is said that the definition of insanity is doing the same thing over and over again and expecting a different result. If you're caught on a negative financial hamster wheel, this book offers a way out. I hope to show you that you can build wealth on your own terms and change your habits around money, which will put you on a path towards financial security and freedom.

Here's to your prosperity!

1

The Hidden Price of an Expensive Life

Mack was raised enjoying an incredibly privileged life funded by her parents—but she didn't realize it back then.

When she was twenty-one, her parents felt it was time for her to make a go of things on her own. They cut her off financially, but she was fine with that. She was excited to prove that she could do things on her own. She landed a well-paying job out of university, but crushing student loans and credit card debt suffocated her efforts at independence. After more than a year trying to make ends meet, she was finally forced, at the age of twenty-nine, to move back home with her parents, who were good enough to take her in. So much for her dream of having her own place and strong finances by the time she was thirty.

Now she feels like she's going backwards as she's stuck watching all of her friends who, with the full financial support of their parents, are sailing through life with their country club memberships, fancy cars, and condos. It's impossible to keep up with them, and the truth is she doesn't want to. What she really wants is to prove she can make it on her own—but how?

WHERE SHE WENT WRONG

Misstep #1: Never Learning the Basics

Growing up, Mack knew money didn't grow on trees, but she really didn't know much else about finances. Her parents paid for everything she needed, plus copious luxuries that she assumed everyone had. She never had a job or an allowance as a teen, and she had a supplementary credit card on her parents' account. For years, her parents had warned that she would be financially cut off once she was twenty-one, but they didn't prepare her for what that meant.

The disturbing fact about financial literacy levels in Canada is that most people rate themselves high when their understanding is quite low. Having a false sense of efficacy could lead you down dangerous paths.

According to a recent report on Canadians' confidence about their financial knowledge:

- 78 percent of Canadians feel they're financially literate.
- 14 percent rate their financial literacy as "excellent."
- 64 percent rate it as "good."

And yet . . .

- 57 percent failed a test on basic financial literacy questions.
- Only 38 percent of women passed (compared to 48 percent of men).

- 52 percent of baby boomers passed.
- 45 percent of Gen X-ers passed.
- 31 percent of millennials passed.[1]

While millennials are most likely to rate their understanding of basic financial literacy as "excellent," they failed the test overwhelmingly. Mack and most millennials are incredibly tech savvy, but their abilities don't always translate into financial sense. This can leave them chasing wants over needs, paying heavily on debt, and ignoring the importance of saving for emergencies and their futures.

Misstep #2: Having No Concept of the Costs of Things

Because Mack never had to use her own money, she never developed a sense of what things cost or the effort that goes into earning an income. In her midtwenties, she once calculated how many hours she would need to work to buy a pricey new designer belt. She realized she'd have to work seventeen hours to afford something that sat in her drawer most of the time—and that didn't include the interest she'd pay if she bought it on a high-interest-rate credit card.

How Much Is That?

When was the last time you calculated how much time you would have to work to buy products or services in your life? In our cashless, tap-and-go society, it's easy to lose touch with how much effort it takes to earn the money that we spend so quickly. And don't forget taxes: if you make $25 per hour, buying something for $25 isn't just an hour of work once you factor in tax, which can range from 15 to 20 percent.

Misstep #3: Keeping Up with the Impossible

Shortly after graduating from university, Mack took six months to backpack around Australia. She saved up a little for the trip and worked odd jobs while she was there to survive. She realized she could be incredibly happy with very little, as she got a taste of the frugal life and found immense joy in activities that cost almost nothing. She took up surfing and yoga on the beach instead of partying and jetting off for expensive ski trips with her school friends. She joined communities of like-minded people who enjoyed living with less and appreciating the bounties of the Australian wilds.

But when Mack got home, her frugal ways went out the window and she found herself trying to live up to the impossible. Her friends and family were all still being funded by their parents and spending money that wasn't their own, and she felt pressured to keep up with them. Naturally, this plummeted her into debt.

Misstep #4: Blowing Her First Credit Limit in One Trip

Just before graduating from university, Mack got her very own credit card. Why not? Who can turn down "free money"? She was approved for $2,500 and she deserved to treat herself! When her friends invited her along for an extended weekend in Whistler, she accepted eagerly. After all, she had this newly found money and it was essentially enough for her flight from Toronto, the ski tickets, and her contribution to the rental car and hotel.

But that credit limit went fast. On the evening before she returned home, Mack offered to buy everyone's dinner and was embarrassed when her card was declined. Sheepishly, she convinced one of her friends to pick up the bill and promised that she'd pay her back later. She had no idea she'd spent as much as she had, and that was just the beginning of her problems. When she got her first statement, she learned the hard way what "minimum payment" really means. There was no way she could pay off the card, and so she was stuck paying off only the interest and carrying a huge balance of unpaid principal. This is when it hit her—there is no such thing as free money or a free trip or even a free lunch. She also suffered a blow to her credit score, one that felt impossible to fix with her minimum payments.

Misstep #5: Not Examining Her Monthly Obligations

Because Mack never learned to properly manage her own money or pay her bills, she never dug into her debts. She had more than $30,000 in student loan debt and three credit cards totalling $25,000, most of them high-interest-rate cards. Her rent set her back more than $2,000 a month, and that didn't include her cable, subscriptions, and cell phone, let alone food or other necessities. These debts piled up quickly and soon she was using one credit card to pay another. She deferred her rent a few months, but the landlord demanded full payment after three.

In order to pay off her late credit card bills, student loan payments, and rent, Mack decided to take out a very costly payday loan. If she had been more financially literate, she would have known to defer some debt with her creditors or even negotiate a better interest rate. It could have bought her a valuable buffer of time and helped her avoid the punishing interest of a payday loan.

Misstep #6: Waiting Too Long to Move Back Home

Mack had vowed she'd never move back home, but she couldn't keep up with the costly bills and heaping student loans. While she was in school, she didn't have to make payments on her loans. But after graduating, she was shocked at how hefty the payments were.

Because Mack ignored her debt, she didn't dig into the government assistance that would have allowed her to defer interest on her government student loans during a time of financial hardship or suspend payments entirely until she was back on solid footing. If she had planned to move home sooner, she could have freed up much-needed income to pay her credit cards on time. She had initially tried to move into a smaller apartment with a lower rent, but her poor credit made it impossible to get approved. Many landlords will request a copy of your credit score, so poor dealings with credit can prevent you from renting as well as buying.

THE SOLUTION

Many of us weren't taught about money in school or even from our parents. But as with any skill you're looking to acquire in life, you need to start with the basics, figure out your blind spots, and understand where you're at—and where you want to be.

Step #1: Learn the Lingo

If you're going to enjoy the money game, you need to start with the basics. Don't be embarrassed if you haven't the foggiest clue about the difference between an RRSP, a TFSA, and a Bitcoin—that's why you're reading this book! The first move towards comprehending anything new is getting a super-clear understanding of the essentials. That way you'll be able to prepare when you're negotiating a mortgage or GIC (guaranteed investment certificate) rate, discussing investments, or getting a loan when you need to finance a new vehicle.

Step #2: Get Organized

Going digital has its perks and more companies are encouraging you to do so. But be sure to set regular calendar reminders to check your statements for accuracy, overcharging, and more.

Once you're organized with your payments and due dates, if you see an income disruption on its way or simply can't meet all of your obligations, get on a call with your creditor at least five to ten business days before the next payment's due date. Keep in mind that automatic payments are set in motion with your creditor and can take several days to be stopped by their system. By getting in touch with your creditor well in advance of your payment due date, you'll be in a much better position to receive a deferral agreement or even an interest rate reduction. You have far less power to negotiate alternative arrangements if you've already missed one or more payments.

When my cell phone provider enticed me to go digital with my statements and initiate automatic payments, I went many months paying my account without checking the statements. It wasn't until a few months later that I realized I was being overbilled by $50 a month. Luckily, the telecom refunded the overpayments, but it could have taken me much longer to notice. Lesson: always check your statements regularly for errors. If you wait longer than thirty to sixty days with your telecom provider or credit card company, you may be left out in the cold if there are fraudulent or incorrect charges. Many won't work with you for a refund past those timelines, but it's still worth calling and seeing what's possible.

If you elect to go paperless with your banking services, it's even more essential that you hop online regularly:

- Check your bank account and credit card accounts every few days. That way, you can clearly see if there was a fraudulent charge or error. It can be tough to remember every purchase at statement time, especially if you have a spouse or teenage child using your accounts as well with a supplementary card. Remember, if you're the primary cardholder, you're on the hook.

- Scour your credit card statements. If you're only paying your minimum payment, your credit card statement will tell you important details like how long it will take you to pay it off. Also check whether there have been any changes to your interest rate if you missed a payment. Most credit card companies will increase your rate if that happens.
- You only have sixty days with most banks to report fraud on your bank or credit card accounts. Stay on top of your purchases and consider setting up transaction alerts through your online banking account. This way, you will receive an email or text each time a transaction is made on your credit card or bank account.

What About Credit Monitoring?

You may have seen credit monitoring services offered by both Equifax and TransUnion, which claim to keep you protected from fraud and identity theft, at the cost of $11.99 to $29.95 per month. But since each lender only pulls one credit report, you'd need to subscribe to both companies' offerings to be fully protected, which could cost you more than $500 a year. You're better off saving the money and checking your own credit regularly. Look into your bank or credit card app, as most allow you to check your score and report for free as often as you'd like.

Be sure to either make a handwritten note of all of your cards or take pictures and email them to yourself. The latter is riskier because if you lose your cell phone, or your computer or your email is hacked, the pictures could be accessed. Memorize your PINs and passwords and never write them down anywhere or share them. If you do and they're used (even by your spouse or child), you may not be covered in the event of fraudulent activity on your account.

Never throw out any documents that have your name, address, account information, or other sensitive details. Fraudsters may physically go through garbage for personal information, and improperly discarded documents will give them exactly what they need to potentially apply for credit in your name. If you don't need to keep a certain document anymore, take care to properly destroy it so it can't be used in the future.

Sadly, "friendly fraud" is an issue as well. That's fraud committed by an ex-spouse, nanny, co-worker, assistant, renovator, or anyone with access to your sensitive information. Keep important documents locked up at home and don't carry your SIN card or leave it lying around anywhere.

What's in Your Wallet?

Check what you're carrying around with you. Do you have more in your wallet and purse than you need?

You should only be carrying:

- One credit card
- One debit card
- Enough cash to get you through a day (more if you're travelling)
- Your health card
- Your driver's licence

Don't carry:

- Your SIN card
- Your birth certificate
- A copy of your passwords

Step #3: Try a Thirty-Day Anti-Budget

I hate budgets. I think they're like diets. Sure, they can produce results in the short term, but in the long term, they can do more harm than good. Instead, try a Thirty-Day Anti-Budget. It's a simple exercise in choice, awareness, and behavioural change.

Thirty-Day Anti-Budget

There are five steps:

1. **Track.** Track every dollar you spend for thirty days. You can write items down or use your bank app to track all of your expenses. Some apps do an excellent job at even breaking down the purchases into categories.

   A note on third-party apps: There are a number of apps on the market that can help you track your finances. However, if they link into your banking or investment accounts and are not your bank app, proceed with caution. While it's convenient to have one app tracking all your financial information, if you use third-party apps, you may nullify the fraud protection offered by your bank and/or credit card company.
2. **Categorize.** Once you have a thirty-day snapshot of your spending, look at the categories where you're spending your money. A financial expert may say you should spend no more than $400 a month on groceries and eating out, but if your family is actually spending $600, that budget is never going to stick. What you're creating here, without judgment, is your baseline of normal spending. Once you're aware of it, you can see areas for improvement and cost-cutting.
3. **Multiply.** Take all of your categories and multiply them by twelve. This gives you an estimate of what you're shelling

out each year per category. You might be surprised by where your money is going. And that's a major point to this exercise. One of my readers shared that when he did this practice, he realized he was spending more than $3,600 a year in Diet Coke—bad for his health and his bank account! He opted for a $200 SodaStream and is still enjoying the benefits.

4. **Trim the excess.** What waste have you identified? Perhaps you're signed up for premium apps or subscriptions that you're not even using? What about lesser identifiable money wasters, such as overpaying on your car or home insurance, too many roaming minutes on your cell plan, or a home phone and cable plan you barely use? If you're enjoying what you're spending your money on, that's great! This exercise is all about choice and awareness. But if small dollars are slipping out of your hands on things that don't bring you joy or utility, this is the time for a recalibration.
5. **Reallocate.** How can your spending be redistributed to serve you better? Logically, if you're like Mack, paying down debt is your first step. But if you're debt-free, perhaps you can use your savings for a much-needed vacation or a rainy-day fund.

Let's look at Mack's Thirty-Day Anti-Budget per month and year:

- Rent: $2,000/$24,000
- Uber: $225/$2,700
- Meal delivery: $320/$3,840
- Dog food/treats/grooming: $180/$2,160
- Wine: $200/$2,400
- Subscriptions: $60/$720
- Cell phone: $90/$1,080
- Groceries: $250/$3,000
- Clothes: $200/$2,400
- Mani-pedis: $90/$1,080
- Unreturned deliveries: $50/$600
- Fancy coffee pods: $100/$1,200
- Interest on loans and credit cards: $520/$6,240
- Balance protector on credit cards: $120/$1,440

If Mack decides to scale back her purchases by 50 percent—by walking when possible instead of taking an Uber, meal planning and cooking more at home, grooming her pooch herself, axing some of the fancy coffee pods in the morning, and sending back the clothes she ordered that didn't fit—she could save $3,255 per year. That's not even breaking a wine night or forgoing her Netflix. Think about how far that could go to paying down her student loan debt and bursting credit card balances. All with little to no sacrifice to her lifestyle, just some serious money mindfulness.

Other Options?

If you prefer not to try my Anti-Budget or are looking for a tune-up in between, a great money mindfulness exercise is to print all of your credit card and bank statements (or gather them if you receive them in the mail). Get out a highlighter and comb through a few months' worth. Highlight the purchases you don't remember buying or using, or that you know got wasted. Add those things up to see the impact of the damage. Then vow to do better, cancel any unused subscriptions, and put those dollars to work elsewhere.

Step #4: Take a Spending Time-Out

If you find yourself chronically overspending, you may need a little time-out. Why not try a dry spending month? Here are a few tips that can help:

- Clear your browser's autofill information so if you've saved your credit card data, it's gone. This helps curb impulse spending. Go to all your retailer accounts and have them purge your credit card, too.
- Unsubscribe from newsletters taunting you with items you desire.
- Leave your credit and debit cards at home when you go window-shopping. Try using cash only and set an amount per week or month. When that's gone, no more spending.
- Instead of impulse buying, make a list of everything you want with dates when you will purchase them (or not). Sometimes setting a future date can help you delay spending now—or you might realize you don't really need the item.

Step #5: Find Some Frugal Friends

Your friends' behaviours can greatly affect your own. If you surround yourself with people who spend money as if it's their last moment on earth, it's pretty hard to resist doing the same. If you want to make a major change in your life, the easiest way is to start to hang around people who are already doing what you want to do. You don't have to divorce your spouse or ditch your bestie, either. Even introducing one friend who challenges you financially can produce big gains. How do they manage their finances? How do they resist temptation? What do they do for pleasure that doesn't involve spending money? Remember: good habits rub off!

If you can't find a real friend (or don't have the time or inclination), signing up for a Facebook or other virtual group can do the trick, too. The idea is to find an accountability buddy who will hold you to your more frugal desires and naturally reinforce your positive behaviour because they do the same with their life.

Step #6: Set Smart Money Goals

If your goal is to become debt-free from your credit card, for example, making a broad statement isn't enough. How will you do it and when?

- If you have, say, $10,000 in credit card debt (at 18.5 percent interest), determine your debt-free day in the future.
- Let's say that date is five years from now. Hop on an online calculator and see what you'd need to do to make it happen.
- Let's assume your monthly payment on that debt is currently around $300. If you continue with those payments, you won't be debt-free for twenty-one years and four months. If

you do the math, to be debt-free in five years, you'll need to pay another $600 per month.

- Now this is super clear, and you can attack this goal by figuring out where you can trim your purchases and redirect the money to these debts.

These might seem like a simple item on your to-do list, but if you chunk it down, there are actually dozens if not more steps. Once you have all the action items broken down, assign a deadline to achieve each, and add it to your online calendar to hold yourself accountable and to give yourself a reminder.

We often don't want to set a goal because we know the chances of not succeeding. Scientists state that 92 percent of people who set New Year's resolutions never achieve them.[2] But don't be afraid of failure or that feeling of guilt when you fail to stay on track or buy something you shouldn't. That's your subconscious reminding you that you made a promise to yourself. Hold yourself accountable and keep working towards your goal.

Reward Positive Behaviour

Unfortunately, when we don't buy that item online that we really want but don't really need, no one pats us on the back. We forgo the instant gratification and receive zero satisfaction in the present. But you can still reward yourself at the end of the week or month. For each thing you don't buy or for each small step you reach in your money goal, add something into a bowl (a paper clip, hairpin, penny) and pat yourself on the back when you see all those add up—a visual reminder of the great work you're doing. Be sure to set up a little reward for yourself at the end of the week or month—a bottle of wine or a decadent latte out, or just watch one of your favourite shows. The cost? Almost nothing.

WHERE IS SHE NOW?

Mack felt so much pity for herself when she first moved back home. But that wasn't going to change her situation. Once she realized what an incredible opportunity this was for a fresh start, she was energized with a newfound positivity.

Mack made a goal to get out of her parents' house in one year, but she also wanted to totally eliminate her credit card debt and reduce her student loan balance by $10,000. It felt like an impossible task, but she broke it down into smaller, more manageable steps.

First, Mack examined her debts and got organized, which turned out to be easier than she thought. She gave herself an internal high five when she logged on to her bank's app and set automatic payments for all of her minimum credit card payments. That way, she'd be sure to not miss a payment. She also set a digital calendar reminder to herself in three months to try upping her minimum payments to a few more dollars, so she could fast-track the payments.

Once she could clearly see what she needed to pay off, it was a matter of figuring out what expenses she could cut and where she could bring in more income. Her payday loan was the first to go. She created a Thirty-Day Anti-Budget that helped her reduce unnecessary purchases, including the costly weekends with her family and friends at the country club. At first, it felt strange to cut some things from her lifestyle, but she was just as happy without them—and she was overjoyed when the steep and dangerous loan was paid off.

She also joined a running group and cycling team. It reminded her of the camaraderie and adventures she'd had in Australia—and the best part was that neither activity cost her anything. Her running and cycling friends didn't drink or party, so she was able to socialize without spending. She still accepted invites from her parents and friends to hang out at the country club, but she found herself visiting them during the day for an inexpensive coffee instead of joining them for lavish dinners. She became mindful about aligning her activities with her new financial goals.

She kept up these new habits, and her one-year goal of moving out, paying off her credit card debt, and knocking down her student loan balance by $10,000 was achieved in just nine months! A few weeks after her thirtieth birthday, Mack signed the lease on a small condo. She finally feels that she's moving forwards and has many goals for the future.

2

Honey, It's *My* Money—Taking Back Financial Control

Lalitha was sailing through life as a marketing exec. She loved her job and spent on every whim. If there was money in her bank account to make it through the month and her credit card wasn't declined, life felt good. Lalitha had been living with her partner, Gerald, for years. Even though she earned more than him, she never had the time for or interest in finance, so she very happily let him be the household's money manager. The two of them had no children, but recently they had got a puppy, which had been quite a learning curve.

Unfortunately, Lalitha had recently learned she was being downsized at her company. The good life, it seemed, had come to a screeching halt. As someone who had worked since her teenage years, she had never spent a moment without a job or income. Even at thirty-six years old, saving had never occurred to her; after all, she was still young. She had decades to worry about that, right?

But after getting laid off from her job, she found herself barely paying her fair share of household expenses, which they'd always agreed to split fifty-fifty. It felt strange to her that she was now in this position, since she'd always earned more than Gerald. Last resorts were her only option. But she didn't know the true price she'd have to pay.

WHERE SHE WENT WRONG

Misstep #1: Deferring Financial Decisions to Her Significant Other

After university, Lalitha moved in with Gerald to save on rent. Even though she made considerably more than him and paid more than her fair share, she deferred all financial decisions to him. That had been the dynamic in her own household growing up: her father handled all the family's money matters. And while her father was happy to answer any financial questions Lalitha had as a young woman, she often felt more overwhelmed and confused after talking to him. She determined that money management was simply something she wasn't good at, and she was happy to let someone else figure it out.

We must remember that it was only about one hundred years ago that women achieved the right to own property in their name. We can't shirk our responsibility to be financially independent because we're busy or because the subject is too intimidating at times. While it may be tempting to neglect your financial responsibilities, rationalizing that you'll get to it later in life, or to abdicate that task entirely to someone else, you're in for a rude awakening if they leave you, mismanage the money, or worse.

Unfortunately, women still aren't stepping up to the financial plate. Even though we've never had more information available, with countless books on finance and easy access to answers on Google, YouTube, and other online platforms, many women prefer to delegate to others.

According to a recent study, women are not owning their wealth, with millennials being the most financially hesitant:

- Half of married women still let their spouse take the lead on long-term financial decisions.
- Nearly half of women with advanced degrees defer to their spouse.
- 41 percent of women who are the primary breadwinners defer to their spouse.
- Women in every industry defer to their spouse—nearly 60 percent in the technology business alone.
- More than 50 percent of millennial women let their spouse handle the long-term financial decisions, compared to 39 percent of boomers.
- Of those millennials deferring, they say that their spouse knows more, that they have no idea where to begin, or that they're too focused on other tasks. Fifty-eight percent simply want to be taken care of—and to keep the peace in the relationship.[1]

There are two other major trends that will impact women's financial security: increasing life expectancy and the rise of "grey divorces," the demographic trend of long-lasting marriages coming to an end later in people's lives. At some point in their life's journey, eight in ten women will find themselves alone and solely responsible for their financial well-being.[2] And if they haven't learned the necessary financial skills already, they will struggle when they can no longer rely on someone else.

Misstep #2: Ignoring Her Credit Score

Lalitha was never interested in watching how much money she earned or saved. Gerald kept track of their joint bills and told her what she owed each month for her share. He even paid her credit cards and student loan payments on her behalf. Lalitha assumed it was all under control and didn't think she needed to re-evaluate her debts or purchases—or to even check that the bills were paid on time or in full, which they almost never were. Confident in Gerald's management, she didn't realize the toll this was all taking on her credit score.

Keeping Up Your Score

It's paramount that you maintain a strong credit rating early in your debt acquisition years (buying a car, home, laptop, etc.). Late payments or high balances can limit your ability to get approved for a mortgage, credit card, or car loan, for example, and can cost you more in interest. Bad credit can take years to repair.

Misstep #3: Earning Well, but Having No Clue Where the Money Was Going—and Never Saving for a Rainy Day

When Lalitha lost her job, the reality of her situation hit her hard. Since she had always spent most of her monthly income, she had never thought to fund an emergency savings account or start investing. She quickly realized her boyfriend wasn't going to be there to help her, since he was just barely getting by himself and also didn't have any savings or a rainy-day fund. She collected some government support after losing her job, but it was far less than her previous income.

Living paycheque to paycheque didn't scare Lalitha. But as soon as that regular income disappeared and weeks passed while she was unemployed, she started to panic. With only a few hundred dollars in her bank account before she lost her job and two maxed-out credit cards, and still bursting with student loan debt, she wasn't set to weather the incoming financial storm. To survive, she ended up getting a third credit card and an increase on one of her other credit cards. Unfortunately, having all that debt and no income caught up to her fast.

Her boyfriend was still using her account to pay her minimum payments, but when there wasn't enough money available, he started paying one every other month. Lalitha didn't know how bad the situation had become until her credit card company started calling her regularly to see when she could make up the missed payments. To make matters worse, Gerald kept pressuring her to cover her back rent, which she was three months behind on.

You can probably imagine the arguments these two had. "How could you let me max out my cards without my even knowing it? How come you didn't pay them off each month?" And Gerald's rebuttals: "How come you never had time to take care of your own finances? How come you're blaming me now when you never seemed to care about our financial picture before?"

Misstep #4: Resorting to Last Resorts

While worrying about how she'd pay the bills, Lalitha saw a number of advertisements for quick cash now. What did she have to lose? She hopped on a call, and the first company she spoke with was super friendly. She told a white lie about having income—after all, she did still have some government money coming in. She couldn't believe how simple and easy the process was. She didn't even have to get out of bed or leave her apartment to get approved! The best part was that she received $1,500 via e-transfer in less than twenty-four hours. This bought her some much-needed breathing room.

But Lalitha failed to read the fine print. This loan had fees and interest of more than 33 percent per month, which equalled just about 400 percent per year. That meant her interest-only payments would be $495 a month. She hadn't had enough to pay her monthly obligations before taking the loan. How was she going to pay that high-interest payment each month *and* attempt to pay the original $1,500 off?

In her mind, there was only one way out: taking a second loan to help pay the first. But soon she found herself spiraling out of control with these terrifyingly high-interest-rate debts.

Misstep #5: Getting Somebody New (and Expensive) to Love

Just before Lalitha lost her job, she and Gerald decided to get a puppy. But neither of them factored in the costs for the new pooch. You can't put a price on (puppy) love, right?

Owning a pet, especially a dog, can be incredibly expensive. According to the ASPCA, the average annual cost of owning a dog is just over $1,000.[3] The American Kennel Club's estimate is even higher—they surveyed one thousand dog owners and found that, on average, owners spent more than $2,000 per year on their dogs.[4] You'll want to budget for expenses such as food, regular vet checkups, training, doggie day care, toys, dog walking, boarding services for when you're away, and unexpected health issues and possibly medication or special care.

THE SOLUTION?

Just as we're always taught to take care of our bodies and health, we must also be mindful of our money and financial health. While it's easy to make the excuse that you're not good at math or don't have the time, it's vital to pay attention to your financial details. If you don't, you risk having to fix problems that can set you back years or decades.

Step #1: Take the Financial Reins

With all of the financial books on the market, free courses, and YouTube videos explaining every concept imaginable, it's never been easier to learn about finance. Depending on a spouse or someone else to make financial decisions on your behalf is a dangerous gamble that can leave you susceptible. Note, too, that if you're a woman putting your trust in a male significant other when it comes to all money matters, there's an extra consideration to ponder long-term: on average, women are divorced at thirty, are widowed at fifty-nine, and live longer than men. Can you see why you absolutely cannot rely on "him" to take total charge of the finances?

When Lalitha hit financial rock bottom, that's when she got serious about turning things around. It wasn't a fun exercise at first, but she gathered up all of her credit card statements and dug into her interest rates and due dates. She added them into her digital calendar with a reminder of at least a week's notice to make sure she made them on time. It's her moment to take control instead of leaving the payments to her boyfriend.

Step #2: Set and Share Your Goals

Research has shown that if you have clear goals, you're much more likely to achieve them.[5] Looking to lose weight and have that desire clearly committed to? Chances are you'll overestimate the calories in a cookie. Invited out to a party but you're dead set on nailing a school paper or work presentation? You're much more likely to overestimate how long the party will last and more likely to opt out.

Share your financial goals with friends to reinforce them, to give your network a chance to support you, and to help hold yourself accountable. If you're trying to go out less because you're saving for your first home, let your loved ones know. Maybe they'll suggest doing a potluck instead of extending a dinner invite to support you on your path.

You should also consider having a professional financial advisor assist you with setting and achieving your goals. A study revealed that Canadians who engage in comprehensive financial planning report significantly higher levels of financial and emotional well-being than those who do none or only limited planning.

Those with comprehensive plans feel:

- more on track with their financial goals and retirement plans (81 percent of those with comprehensive financial plans feel on track with their financial affairs, versus 73 percent with limited planning, and only 44 percent with no planning)
- able to save more (62 percent of those with comprehensive financial plans report that they have improved their ability to save in the last five years, versus 56 percent with limited planning, and only 40 percent with no planning)
- more confident about facing financial challenges
- better able to indulge in discretionary spending on occasion[6]

If Lalitha had a robust rainy-day fund and lots of room on her credit cards for an emergency, she could have lessened the blow of suddenly losing her job. Ideally, she could have also had a low-interest-rate line of credit that would have given her an extra cushion while she pivoted into a new job or field.

Step #3: Keep Your Credit Clean

It's pretty hard to navigate today's world without credit. You need a major credit card for everything from purchasing plane tickets to making a hotel reservation. It's true that you can do more and more with your debit card, but you don't get any of the protections that you do with a credit card.

Credit Score 101

It's crucial to be aware of your credit score. The good and bad news about your score is that it changes every month. Do the right thing and your score stays high or improves. Make the wrong moves and it can tank quickly. There are obvious times you'll want your score as high as possible, such as when you're applying for a loan, mortgage, line of credit, or credit card. But there are also less obvious times, like when you're applying for a job, an apartment, a new cell phone, or a laptop lease. Depending on your province, many home and auto insurance policies use your credit score when determining your rate.

You might be wondering what your score is all about. It's a proprietary measurement by both of the credit reporting agencies in Canada—Equifax and TransUnion—that gives a snapshot of how you've managed your debt.

Credit scores in Canada range from 300 to 900, with higher being better. It's estimated that only 5 percent of Canadians have a score of 850 or higher. While your score is important, it's really the "bands" of scores that lenders care about. Most often, the bands look like this:

833–900	Excellent
790–832	Very good
743–789	Good
693–742	Fair
300–692	Poor

You can see that whether you have a score of 744 or 780, it's still only considered "good." It's not until you reach 790 or above that you move into the "very good" band. Generally, you need a credit score of 760 or higher to qualify for the best rates at a bank.

Don't get too concerned if you check your score for the first time and it's less than stellar. It could be that there's something incorrect on your credit report or that you accidentally have something sitting in collections. When people move or close an account, there may be an owed amount that gets sent off to collections, and that can severely impact your score, even if the amount is super small. Or perhaps you have fallen behind a few times on credit payments. Again, not to fret. With consistent positive behaviours, you can get your score up in around six months or a year for even some of the worst scores (not including bankruptcy or credit proposals).

What's a credit report and what's on it?

Your credit report is a snapshot of what credit you have and how you've handled it. It does not include your assets, net worth, or salary, so it's only one component of the criteria that a lender uses when considering approving you for new debt—but it's an especially important one.

You'll find the following on your report:

- Your name, social insurance number, address, and possibly employment details—what you likely provided to your last lender.
- A list of all of your debts, your last reported balances, your limits, how many times you've been late on payments, how late your accounts have been, and how long you've had your debt.
- For late payments, it will list how many times you've been thirty, sixty, or ninety days late.
- Any times that you've stopped paying a debt and it went into collections.
- If you've filed for bankruptcy or a consumer proposal.
- Who's looking at your credit file, divided into soft and hard inquiries. A hard inquiry is when you apply for credit. You agree to your report's being accessed, and it can temporarily hurt your score, especially if you have too many inquiries at one time. A soft inquiry is when your report is accessed but it doesn't affect your score. For example, your existing credit card company may peek into your report to see if it wants to increase or decrease your limit. When you check your own credit report, this would also show as a soft inquiry. I want to underscore that it *does not* affect your credit at all when you check your report or score. You could do it every day if you wanted and it wouldn't impact it at all.

What's reported, what's not?

Generally speaking, all of your debts and some of your financial obligations are listed on your report, such as from:

- credit cards
- loans
- lines of credit
- mortgages
- rent payments
- cell phone payments
- collection accounts

It's crucial to note that a creditor doesn't have to report your payments. It is possible that your bank doesn't report your mortgage, your landlord doesn't report your rent, or your cell phone provider doesn't report your payments. However, that could always change in the future, so the best strategy is to pay everything on time every month.

What's not on your report?

Your electricity and hydro payments or auto and home insurance won't be reported unless they go into collections.

Generally, if you're behind a month or two with your bills, you can make payment arrangements with the lender or service provider. Once you haven't made a payment for at least ninety days, the lender or provider will often write off the owed amount and sell the file to a collection agency to try to get you to pay your outstanding balance. Those collections filed on your report can be difficult to have removed and can affect your score negatively. So, you'll want to do all you can to not have an overdue bill move into collections.

What impacts your score?

Every credit file and situation is unique. But generally, the following affects your score:

Payments

How often you're on time or late on your payments will have an impact on your score, as well as how many times you've been late more than thirty, sixty, or ninety days. Having one ninety-days-late payment is worse than having three thirty-days-late payments.

Utilization

"Utilization" refers to how much credit you've used. If, for example, you have a $10,000 credit limit on a card and have a balance of $2,000, your utilization is 20 percent. If you pay it off entirely before the due date, then it drops back to 0 percent. But if you carry a $2,000 balance each month, for example, you're at 20 percent each month. Ideally, you never want to be over 50 percent, and zero is best. There is a myth that carrying any type of balance is good for your score because it shows that you're using your debt, but this isn't true.

You can't guarantee when your lender reports to the credit agency, but generally your credit card company reports to the credit bureaus on your statement date. Let's look at an example:

You have a $10,000 limit on your credit card. You came back from a big family trip and have $4,000 on your card. Your due date is March 4 and you pay it in full. That's great! That means you won't be paying any interest to the credit card company and you were on time with your payment. So that's one check mark for you.

But let's say that your next statement is generated by your credit card company on March 22, with a payment due date of April 4. Let's also pretend that on March 21, you were finishing a little reno and paid the floor installer $5,000 on your credit card.

It's no big deal, since you don't have to pay it off until April 4, right? Well, since March 22 is the statement date—when your credit card company generated what you owed for the month—that's the date that it will likely report to the credit bureaus, and now they'll see you have a utilization of 50 percent.

If you're not concerned about your credit score, this issue isn't a major one. But if you are watching your score or trying to improve it, it can make a big difference. So, the takeaway is: if you're trying to improve your score, you need to be aware of two dates with your revolving credit—the due date and the statement date. Make sure you're on time paying with your due date and have as little as possible on your card on the statement date.

Utilization only counts with revolving credit. "Revolving" means that you can use it or pay it down anytime. This includes lines of credit (secured or not) and credit cards. It does not include loans, mortgages, or your cell phone. If you have no control over the payment you make (it's fixed), then it's not revolving and utilization for purposes of your score doesn't matter.

Finally, keep in mind that if you're maxed out on your credit card (using nearly $10,000 on your $10,000-limit card), that's a huge red flag and will drag your score down or keep it low. It basically sends a message that you might be in trouble, might be unable to pay your debts, and could possibly default. If you're only maxed out one month out of a couple of years, it likely won't make a difference. But if it's a pattern, it will affect your score. Even if you're consistently using only about 20 percent or 30 percent of your limit, that can still send a message that you're not managing your debt well because you're not paying it off every month.

Length of time you've had your debt

The longer the history you have with your debt, the more it will positively affect your score. If you have a credit card that you've had for some time that you don't need, for purposes of keeping your score high, you're better off keeping it and using it regularly for small-ticket items like filling up your gas tank, and then paying it off immediately.

The type and mix of debt you have

If all you had was a cell phone bill on your credit report, it wouldn't build your score very quickly. Ideally you should have a mix of credit cards, loans, maybe a line of credit, and a mortgage. It may take time and patience to get to this point, so don't be frustrated if you're just starting out.

How much credit you have outstanding

You could have a number of accounts with a zero balance on them but also a less-than-stellar credit score if you simply have too much revolving credit open. Again, it depends on your unique situation, but more isn't always better. Having too many credit cards with large limits means that you could rack them up tomorrow, even if you never intend on doing so.

How often you're applying for credit

Generally speaking, applying for too much credit in a short amount of time can have the credit bureau's algorithm seeing red. This can happen innocently enough. Say you're moving to a new city. You apply for a car loan, your landlord checks your credit, and then you apply for a new cell phone, and whammy—you're declined on the last one. Why? It can seem to the algorithm that you're in trouble and trying to get a bunch of credit fast. This might not be the case at all. However, it's best that you spread out new applications for credit to avoid getting declined and a hit to your score.

What If You Have a Payment Dispute?

If you rent, lease, or have a loan on an asset and later have a disagreement with the seller, continue to pay your payments on time during the disagreement. Let's say you leased a laptop and had nothing but problems and the company is doing a poor job servicing your issues. Perhaps you send it back, demand a new one, and refuse to pay your lease payments until you receive satisfaction. I would feel your pain but would caution you to still pay your agreed-upon payments. If you do, and you're in the right, you can go after the company later to recoup your payments. But if you're in the wrong or the issues never get resolved, they will report the late payments on your credit file and technically it will be accurate. Even in a dispute, make your payments on time and try to collect or rectify the situation separately.

When Lalitha was finally brave enough to check her credit score on her bank app, a pit welled up in her stomach. It was just about as bad as it could get: 525. She read through what was keeping her score low, and the report stated that her missed payments and one old cell phone bill for $50 that was in collections were the problems. She was determined to find a new job and tackle her debt along with getting her score up. But first, Lalitha needed to contact her old telecom company and pay off her outstanding balance. Once that was out of collections, her score would start to increase.

Step #4: Get Help Before You Need It

If you can't make your credit card, loan, or mortgage payment; keep up with your utilities; or even stick with the payment arrangements you've made with Canada Revenue Agency (CRA) for your back taxes, staying silent is your least effective strategy. If you miss payments, your creditors have to make their own assumptions and will usually come to the worst conclusion—that you're not going to pay. This could mean your cell phone or heat getting cut off, or your car or home being repossessed. The CRA can take swift legal action and garnishee your bank accounts and more.

Most creditors will work with you if you're proactive and keep the lines of communication open. And by letting them know your situation, you give them the opportunity to present solutions you didn't know existed, like deferring payments or making interest-only payments until you get back on your feet.

But don't wait until you've missed payments to make a deferral arrangement. Once you do, your creditor will be much less likely to work with you. And get ahead of the payment date, assuming deferrals take five or more business days to implement. If you call the day before the due date, there may be no way for them to stop the payment, resulting in costly nonsufficient funds (NSF) fees and a less flexible creditor.

Red flags that you need help include:

- Missing payments
- Paying only minimum payments on your credit cards continuously
- Using one form of debt to pay for another
- Taking costly cash advances from your credit cards to pay for necessities or other obligations
- Using very expensive payday loans (upwards of 400 to 600 percent annually depending on your province)
- Cashing in investments or RRSPs
- Creditors or collection agencies are calling

You can absolutely negotiate help with your lenders directly, but if you're simply unable to or too stressed by the situation, reach out for advice and guidance from a non-profit credit counsellor or insolvency trustee.

If Lalitha had been on top of her debts and due dates, she could have deferred her payments with her creditors or moved into a lower-rate credit card. But because she waited until she had missed a few payments, they wouldn't consider her request until she had made at least six months of payments on time.

Step #5: Research the Costs of Pets Before You Commit

Even knowing the costs of her puppy, Lalitha would have likely got him anyway. We can't blame her, can we? But with a new fur baby comes financial commitments. You need to have a separate emergency account and/or consider getting pet insurance. There's nothing worse than being in a dire financial situation and not being able to get your furry buddy the medical attention it needs in the case of an emergency.

You should budget upwards of $2,000 a year in a safe, easily accessible bank account. Ideally, you should have this available before you make the commitment to get a new pet. And depending on the breed and its possible genetic predispositions, you may need much more. It's not uncommon for pet surgeries to run $5,000 or even $10,000, in addition to medication and rehabilitation.

When researching pet insurance, be aware of deductibles—whether you have to pay out of pocket first—the ability to choose your own vet, and much more. Weigh the pros and cons of having coverage versus self-insuring by saving up for possible emergencies yourself.

WHERE IS SHE NOW?

Lalitha hated being unemployed. It was such a blow to her self-esteem and finances. She had never been in financial trouble before and vowed it would never, ever happen again. Looking back, she can't believe that she let her partner look after the finances. She's reminded of the expression "What you appreciate appreciates." And she'll never ignore her money or debt again.

After Lalitha landed an even better job as a marketing executive with a utility company, she enrolled in a financial literacy class online and bought a few books on the subject. Armed with the basics, she started to dip her toes in the financial waters. She opened a TFSA and an RRSP with a robo-advisor and never missed the monthly $100 she invested in both plans. She also looked at her monthly financial obligations and determined that she could afford allocating $600 a month to fast-track paying off her credit cards. With the $600 monthly, she could be debt-free in as little as five years. But she wanted to take it further.

She watched a video on habit-stacking and decided to apply it to her financial life. Each morning, as soon as she sat down with her cup of coffee, she checked her bank and investing apps. If she spent on her credit card one day, she immediately moved that amount of money over from her savings account to pay the balance. Although she had all her debt due dates in her digital calendar, she wasn't going to wait until it was time to pay—she paid before the deadline.

Over time, her seemingly insignificant savings of $200 a month added up to more than $8,500. She was starting to get how positively addictive it could be to pay attention to your money and grow your wealth.

Shortly after Lalitha began her new job, Gerald left her to return home to his native England. Although her heart was broken, she at least wasn't in financial ruin. She knew she could take care of her own finances and didn't need anyone to do that for her in the future.

Now, after some time has passed, Lalitha's thinking about dating. But it's actually not her top concern. She has the company of her dog, and while she has to pay the living expenses all by herself, she's become such a good saver that she manages all of the expenses easily. And she enjoys the free time she has to do her own thing. Moreover, with a robust emergency savings account, a positive savings trajectory, and zero credit card debt, Lalitha feels financially empowered.

She Who Talks Money, Earns Money

Eva was fuming after her boss, Julie, told her she had yet again been passed up for a salary increase. She'd been working for this non-profit organization for more than four years and hadn't received one raise or perk. When she had her fundraising hat on, she was a shrewd negotiator, yet whenever she tried to talk salary and Julie blew her off, Eva felt totally defeated. How could she be a tiger for the organization and a scared turtle when it came to advocating for herself?

Eva didn't only feel like a doormat at work. She let her friends walk all over her, too. When she bought everyone drinks, lunches, and even dinners, she expected the favours to be repaid, but they never were. So why did Eva keep doing the same things over and over, and what was the real cost—to Eva and to her bottom line?

Eva had nearly zero savings even though she was in her midfifties.

She didn't see the point of her money just sitting in an account when she could use it for her wants and desires now.

WHERE SHE WENT WRONG

Eva was allowing emotional blackmail to lead her financial life. She hoped for different outcomes with her boss and co-workers, but she was afraid to actually say anything for fear she'd be labeled "difficult," "demanding" . . . or something much worse. Fact: men take more corporate risks, and their often hard-wired propensity to believe in their work is financially rewarded.

Misstep #1: Feeling That If She Just Did the Work, She'd Get Noticed and Reap the Reward

A 2012 survey conducted by Bullhorn Inc. found that 54 percent of women worked more than nine hours per day, compared to 41 percent of men.[1] The survey also found that women were more likely to do work on vacation and less likely to abuse their sick leave.

Eva was being paid for 40 hours of work per week, but she worked far more than that. Why? Because she wanted to do a good job and she thought the executives would take notice. But they didn't, and she couldn't get that time back. Eva earned $67,000 a year gross (before taxes), which equates to roughly $30 an hour if she worked an average 40-hour workweek, never taking any time off. She worked an extra 15 hours per week at her job, which equals 780 unpaid hours per year, or $23,400. If you add up her volunteer hours with her company, that's another 10 hours per week, 520 unpaid hours per year, and $15,600 in unpaid time. Not only did she not receive the raise she desired, she gave the organization just about half a year's worth of her annual salary in time *for free*.

Volunteering is a wonderful act of generosity with your most precious resource: time. Whether you're considering serving on a committee or an unpaid board, or simply delivering meals or groceries to seniors, giving of your time can fill your life with richness and your heart with joy. But if the time you're giving is at work and not for a charitable reason, consider a rethink—especially when your extra efforts are being overlooked. Eva assumed volunteering for numerous projects at work would eventually result in a raise. She couldn't have been more wrong.

Misstep #2: Not Putting Her Requests Down in Writing

Research by Accenture found that only 45 percent of women are willing to ask for a raise, compared to 61 percent of men, which may explain much of the salary differences between men and women.[2] It's estimated that women are leaving as much as $1.5 million on the table during their working careers simply by not asking for a raise.

Eva approached her boss about a raise and promotion every few months, but she never made her demands known in writing. Therefore, she didn't have a digital paper trail or time stamps for her requests.

Misstep #3: Being Afraid to Escalate Matters

When Eva was negotiating for the non-profit, she was strong, confident, and didn't stop until she got results. Yet, when it came to dealing with her boss, Julie, she felt small and scared and didn't want to upset her. She knew if she could make her case to the CEO, she'd very likely get a raise, but she was afraid of upsetting Julie. She worried that if she pushed too hard, it would backfire and create tension in her day-to-day work relationship with Julie or even get her fired.

Women are far more likely to let these fears stand in the way of having difficult conversations. But it's those conversations that make a real financial difference—something that men quite often seem to understand better than women.

Misstep #4: Always Wanting to Appear Generous

Eva wasn't sure why she always picked up the tab when she and her friends went out for a night on the town. It was as if it were hard-wired deep in the recesses of her psyche. Perhaps it was because her mom always did the same thing with her friends? But lurking deep in her veins was a bubbling resentment. Eva always felt let down when her friends didn't reciprocate her generosity.

The reciprocity rule is hard-wired in our brains: when we do something for someone else, whether we're conscious of it or not, we keep score. We expect the favour to be returned. But when it never is, that's when it's time to consider what a friendship is and isn't. Eva's generosity was being taken advantage of. It's that simple.

Misstep #5: Not Recognizing the Impact of Financial Trauma on Her Decision-Making

Growing up, Eva's brothers regularly raided her piggy bank. She always felt like her money was all gone before she got a chance to enjoy it, so now she didn't save at all. What was the point if the money was just going to disappear? As an adult, she found herself remembering these incidents often, and her view of savings could be traced to these formative memories.

Think about when you were five or ten years old. How did you view money? Was it plentiful, easy to come by? Or was it hard to find, always a struggle for your family? Did you ever feel cheated by family members or siblings? Were you worried about financial matters? Were you taught to spend or to save? How did your early experiences impact your behaviours around money?

When I apply these questions to myself, I can't help but recall my struggling single mother, who worked so hard to care for me and my siblings. Most nights she would be ironing something in the basement, and I'd sit on the stairs shooting the breeze with her. She loved spray starch, and everything had to be perfectly pressed. Sometimes, my mom would take me to the bank when she would cash her paycheque. She always insisted on receiving fresh bills, rejecting the old, tattered ones.

Every few months, my mom and I visited one of my uncles, who would give me a folded-up fifty-dollar bill at the end of our time together. To a young kid, getting that burnt-orange note was like winning a lottery. I'd rush home, plug in the iron (Gen X kids had less supervision with hot appliances), and press the bill until it was perfect. (This was long before our paper bills became plastic.)

I can still recall the wonderful scent of that starchy money! You might think I'm telling you this to brag about what a good saver I was at a young age, but alas, I wasn't. I made all the missteps, too! That money I so carefully ironed was already pre-spent in my mind on candy and clothes. Yes, that's right. I ironed the bill only to then go to the store and spend all of it, all at once. A lot like Eva, I believed that it was better to spend than to save, a habit I later had to break out of to become a financially secure adult.

What I'm saying here is not that spending is bad and saving is good, but that balance is everything, and understanding the impact of early childhood experiences around money is the first step in challenging your own assumptions.

Misstep #6: Worrying Too Much About the Future to Risk a Career Change

Eva was a die-hard Gen X-er. Loyalty to her organization had been instilled in her by her baby boomer bosses and co-workers early in her career. Even so, she'd had colleagues who had to move laterally in order to get the pay they deserved. But whenever she thought about leaving her job, she felt guilty. And it was that guilt that stopped her from applying for a higher-paying job elsewhere.

According to a recent study carried out by CareerBuilder, 29 percent of respondents say they regularly search for new jobs while they're employed.[3] A whopping 78 percent say they're open to trying something new if a good opportunity arises.[4] And 54 percent of workers favour switching to a new company after less than two years in a job.[5]

Eva secretly checked recruiters' listings for new jobs but never applied for them. She was worried that a move would look bad on her résumé, so she stayed put, hoping her efforts would one day be recognized by her boss.

Waiting for a Dream?

If you've ever dreamed of leaving your job for a better and higher-paid one, you're not alone. A recent survey found that 54 percent of women fantasize at least once a month about quitting their job, while 16 percent fantasize every day about leaving![6] What's important, though, is to know why you're fantasizing and what you're missing in your current role, and then making a clear decision that promotes a strong financial future. It's okay to daydream for a while, but if you're truly unhappy with your rate of pay and you can't see a strong future in your company, then it's time to turn fantasy into reality instead of just dreaming away your career.

THE SOLUTION?

I don't think I've ever met a woman, tough or meek, who isn't better at (and more comfortable) standing up for someone else rather than for herself. There's nothing wrong with lifting others up. It's an act of generosity. But at the same time, you need to put the emergency mask on yourself first, breathe in the oxygen deeply, and start to advocate for yourself as if you were your own best friend.

Let's look at how Eva can keep her generous heart but also campaign for recognition of her exceptional work and her worth.

Step #1: Toot Your Own Horn

I know women—from those starting out to those very senior in their career—who tell me that they don't want to seem boastful or overconfident and that self-advocating makes them feel both. Self-advocating and calling out your achievements is not an exercise in ego gratification. In our fast-paced world, you need to speak up for your accomplishments. Your boss is as busy and overwhelmed as you are. Don't expect others to take the time to pat you on your back and acknowledge what you've produced.

Make a habit of recording your accomplishments, and at appropriate times, share these results with your boss. And when I'm talking about self-advocating, I don't mean creating a lot of fluff on Instagram. That's not going to get your boss to give you a raise or help you land that great job with the higher salary and more interesting role. LinkedIn, however, is one place where you might consider building a professional profile. You can use it as a database of your achievements. You can share career-based research and articles, thereby drawing attention to your own interests, capabilities, and thought leadership.

Eva's workplace set deadlines and benchmarks all the time. She had projects due at certain times and had measurable sales targets she had to meet. So why was it that whenever she talked to her boss, Julie, about a raise, the bar always moved? "Let's examine that in six months," or "I know I said six months, but now let's see if the company increases profits by twenty percent in another six months."

Don't fall prey to this tactic. Keep an ongoing paper or digital diary of your daily, weekly, monthly, and yearly accomplishments. Remind your boss of the blood, sweat, and maybe even tears that went into each. And hold your boss accountable to a timeline about your salary review. Politely call out the tactic if you get stalled, and if you have to, politely propose your own deadline. "Six months is a long time to wait, and I recall that I've waited before. I'd really like to review this sooner. Can we discuss it when my next project is complete in five weeks? That should provide more measurable benchmarks for us both."

If you're really stymied and can't seem to get a raise despite several attempts at discussion, maybe it's time for a lateral move to a new job. Perhaps another employer will see your skills for what they are and pay accordingly. Make sure to weigh apples and oranges, though. Consider health and pension benefits, vacation time, room for advancement, and the overall financial health of any potential new workplace.

Enlist the Help of Advocates

If you really struggle to advocate for yourself, you might want to start a strategic mastermind group with a few other women. Organize a group of like-minded individuals who can challenge your thinking. The ideal group size is around a dozen. Set goals for yourself, which you'll share with others. Meet monthly and keep the focus of the meetings on supporting and promoting each other's career efforts.

Step #2: Always Put It in Writing

It's one thing to make a request verbally; it's another thing to do it in writing. It's easy for a boss to simply ignore a verbal request, but when something is in writing, that's another matter altogether.

This is as important for your boss as it is for you. A paper trail will make you more conscious of your own goals and of the timeline. How long has it been since you last asked for a raise? If you check your paper trail, you'll know exactly—and quite often, you'll be surprised how much time has passed since your last request.

When asking for a meeting to discuss promotions and raises, you might do so verbally, but always follow up in writing afterwards. If you don't receive a timely reply, politely follow up at least twice. If you still get blown off, consider going to your boss's boss. If that's not possible, it may be necessary to look for new opportunities elsewhere. Your financial future depends on it.

Step #3: Curb Your Financial Generosity If It's Underappreciated

A brilliant speaker I once heard offered an elegant and magnificent solution to honouring your goals, wants, and desires while respecting your time. When someone asks you to do something you don't have time for or simply don't want to do, just say no gently and then—here's the most important part—*stop talking*. Often, that's enough, and if you don't stop talking you might find yourself changing your answer when you really can't afford to take on another request.

Here's a personal example. A few years ago, a client I was working with invited me to write a series of free articles for their start-up business. I made the mistake of *not* saying "No, thank you" immediately. Instead, I offered reasons why I couldn't do it and simply didn't have the time. The next thing I knew, I was browbeaten into writing "just a couple." But this was a terrible use of time. Also, I wasn't paid for my work! Learn from me and say no once, properly, rather than committing to doing something that's a financial and time burden.

For Eva, saying no meant no longer paying for everything. If you get into a bad generosity habit like Eva did when the bill came, it's time for a brave money conversation with your friends or co-workers. Eva could start a typical dinner out by saying to the server, "I'm getting the first round of drinks, but after that, it will be separate bills, thanks." Or simply, "It's separate bills tonight, thanks." Once she nails that, she may even be able to ask for what's fair in the future: "Remember that I've been paying the bill for the last year? I was happy to, but can someone else take it tonight?"

You'll be amazed how, with a bit of practice, you'll start to feel more confident about setting financial boundaries. And when you look at your credit card bill at the end of the month, you'll really sit up taller.

Step #4: Say Yes to the Right Ask, Not to Everything

There's plenty of research out there that suggests women will put their hands up to do more work more often than men will at the workplace. Before you agree to adding to your workload, take a moment to consider whether accepting this task:

- will lead to new skills you wish to acquire
- will allow you to increase your corporate visibility (such as chairing a notable committee)
- will result in a gain in experience or networking opportunities
- is likely to end in some kind of long- or short-term financial gain

Step #5: Make a Time Budget

Your time is finite and has a monetary value. Making a time budget helps you become conscious of how you spend your time. In finance, we talk about "opportunity costs." If you pursue one opportunity, it's often at the expense of another, so choose wisely! The same logic applies to your time. If you spend time doing one thing, it means not having time to do another.

To make a time budget, add up how much time you spend sleeping, working, commuting, and doing other non-negotiables (such as cooking, exercising, or enjoying moments with friends/family). What you have left is the time you can use for yourself.

Make a list now of the following:

- All your current and desired extracurricular activities
- What you want to accomplish this month, quarter, and year

Once you see how little time you have left in a week, month, or year, you'll need to decide how much you want to give to working for free. Remember that when you're giving away your time for free, it's coming out of your "you time" budget.

Once it's clear how much time you have and what you want to accomplish with it, consider setting clear goals to hold yourself accountable. Change takes time, of course, but the first step is to see your own time as precious and valuable—a currency in and of itself.

Step #6: Jump Ship When the Time Is Right

Eva held a false belief: that switching jobs would look bad on her résumé and make her undesirable to future employers. That's simply not the case today. Lateral moves can be financially lucrative, though it does take bravery and work to find the best fit. Shockingly, some studies even show that remaining employed at a company for longer than two years can decrease your lifetime earnings, whereas changing jobs every few years will pay off financially over time.[7] Eva stuck it out at her job. She did everything to get a raise, and yet she was still being denied and ignored.

Finally, she decided that if nothing changed soon, she'd test the waters elsewhere and start a job hunt. If you're in a similar struggle to Eva's, first see if there are opportunities for advancement at your company before considering switching careers. The unfortunate truth is that women are conditioned to think they need every box ticked before stretching for a higher-paying or more powerful position. According to a study by Hewlett-Packard, men will apply for a job when they feel they're about 60 percent qualified. But women? They don't typically apply until they are 100 percent certain they are qualified.[8]

WHERE IS SHE NOW?

Before applying to other jobs, Eva tried one last time to ask her boss for a raise. She emailed her request and Julie agreed to a meeting a month away. A day before they were to connect, Julie cancelled out of the blue. When Eva asked to reschedule, Julie pushed her request out several months, citing a big project that was taking up a lot of her time.

The writing was on the wall. Julie's continued rejection was the push Eva needed to conduct a proper job search. She started by refreshing her LinkedIn profile. Next, she worked with a hired pro to spruce up her outdated résumé. The process had her excited; she was finally going to stop fantasizing and do something productive.

She consulted with some good friends—the kind who pay their

own way and have "been there, done that" when it comes to lateral moves. Their cheerleading and tough love about negotiations helped Eva persist. It wasn't easy to navigate the crowded job-search market, but Eva was determined. Her friends helped her write a killer cover letter and made some helpful suggestions about her résumé. They could see skills and accomplishments that she herself had diminished or omitted.

Eva was delighted when she received some calls from potential employers. She went to three interviews that went okay, but she was still out of practice and not great at selling herself. With a bit of help from her friends, she nailed the fourth interview, only to be disappointed that she didn't land the job. But five was her lucky number. She hit the career jackpot and landed her dream job, a step up in terms of responsibility but nothing she couldn't handle.

Now she's happily working in a new firm with a salary 20 percent higher than what she was paid at her last job. Her boss never misses a check-in. Eva's been there a year now, and guess what? Her boss came to *her* to say it was time for a raise. Funny how confidence breeds success . . . and more money.

4

I Never Said "I Do" to Your Debt

When Annie was in her twenties and moved out of her family home, her mom and dad surprised her with an incredibly special gift. They gave her a 20 percent down payment to buy her first condo and co-signed the mortgage so she could get approved. Annie poured her savings from working several jobs during her teen years into the condo.

When Annie went abroad to get her MBA, she rented out her condo. While away at school, she racked up huge student loan debt . . . and she met the love of her life, Ritu.

Feeling homesick after graduation, Annie headed back to Vancouver because her tenant's lease was up. Ritu tagged along. "That's cool," Annie said. "Where will you live?"

Ritu's answer: "With you, of course."

Let's face it: people in love make mistakes. Annie wasn't keen on this idea because they hadn't been together for very long, but she didn't say no, and Ritu moved into Annie's condo with her.

Annie landed an excellent job at a big bank and climbed the

corporate ladder. The pay was more than she'd imagined, but she also had a six-figure student loan and the condo's mortgage. Ritu, meanwhile, was having a grand old time in a new city and didn't seem terrifically eager to land a job. Annie's salary wasn't extending nearly as far as it should have, what with a freeloader at home.

Time went by. A year, then two. And then one more. Ritu, all the while, struggled to find consistent work. She made excuses, and though she helped with the dishes, most of her days were spent watching TV or playing video games.

At long last, Annie had had enough. "Look," she said. "You have to find a permanent job or move out."

"I could have done that long ago if I had a car," Ritu argued. "Do you know what the job market is like? There are lots of jobs that require a vehicle, which I don't have."

That's when Annie got her "bright idea." She saw her chance to get Ritu off the couch. She co-signed a loan from a secondary lender to buy her some wheels. Did this mean Ritu landed a great job? No.

Things got tense between Annie and Ritu after that. Annie even went home to her parents for a bit because she just couldn't deal with Ritu anymore. Over their months apart, Annie had a number of calls and meetings with Ritu and hinted that she was going to move back to her condo and that she was fairly sure the relationship was over.

Ritu, meanwhile, just before Annie was moving back to her home, served her with a lawsuit for half the condo and full ownership of the car she'd bought. Gobsmacked, Annie wondered how this could happen. She wasn't even married to Ritu. She'd just crashed with Annie all those years ago and Annie could never get rid of her. Annie had supported her because she thought that's what you do—you help your partner out of a rut—but now Ritu was using Annie's patience and goodwill against her.

WHERE SHE WENT WRONG

Annie wasn't alone in thinking that moving in with someone isn't a big deal. But marriage isn't the only union that bonds a couple financially. Her goodwill towards Ritu and financial support actually created a scenario where she was now potentially legally Ritu's provider and Ritu was her dependent.

Misstep #1: Moving in Without an Agreement

Annie let a lot of time pass in her relationship without realizing she was slipping towards a legal union. She wouldn't have dreamed of getting married without first discussing finances and ensuring they were on the same page, yet she didn't understand the ramifications of common-law cohabitation.

Common law differs in each province. In Ontario, for example, two people are considered common-law partners if they have been continuously living together in a conjugal relationship for at least three years.[1] If they have a child together by birth or adoption, then they only need to have been living together for one year. That said, a common-law relationship in Ontario does not necessarily give rise to property rights—typically just spousal or child support obligations. However, Annie is living in British Columbia, where common-law couples *are* subject to division of family property.

Misstep #2: Co-signing Without Thinking

Annie's intentions were noble when she co-signed for a car and loan for Ritu. Ritu assured her that it would allow her to finally get a job and that she'd make all of the payments.

If a friend, partner, or child needs credit, it's natural to want to help out. But a verbal agreement by one party to make the payments won't stand up in the case of default with the lender or if the issue goes to court.

Annie didn't factor in the possibility that Ritu's defaulting on her promises would mean *she* was on the hook for Ritu's payments. Worse, if she didn't cover the monthly obligation, it was her credit rating on the line. Annie never thought her generosity could bite her back as it did. She assumed if Ritu stopped making payments the most she'd be responsible for was half. The reality? She's totally responsible for all debts she co-signed on.

Misstep #3: Getting a Designer Degree (Cost of Schooling Abroad)

The costs of postsecondary schooling increase every year. To determine the real price of an education in Canada, in 2017 *Maclean's* undertook a first-ever survey of 23,384 undergraduate students to find out how they spend their money—and how they saved for an education.[2] It found the average cost of a year of postsecondary education in Canada is $19,498.75. But for some students, the amount is significantly higher. A University of Toronto student living off campus can expect to spend $23,485 each year, the highest average amount in the survey. Second on the list was Ryerson at $23,066, followed by Saint Mary's University in Halifax at $22,892. Meanwhile, students living at home and attending Sherbrooke had the lowest cost for an education, at just $4,284.

The average Canadian university graduate finishes school with about $15,500 in student debt.[3] An average MBA program in the US is $60,000 to $90,000, compared to $20,000 to $22,000 on average in Canada.[4] That doesn't include housing, books, living expenses, or the exchange rate. And that debt can be debilitating. According to an eight-year study by independent personal insolvency firm Hoyes, Michalos & Associates Inc., approximately

22,000 ex-students filed for bankruptcy in 2018 to address their student debt.[5]

Instead of attending a school in Canada, which would have been much cheaper, Annie opted for a program in the US. That program cost her more than $220,000, including her living expenses (in Canadian dollars converted from US costs), and she returned home with $180,000 in student loan debt.

Misstep #4: Leaving Domestic Dollars on the Table (Bursaries and Grants in Canada)

By choosing schooling abroad, Annie failed to take advantage of money in the form of grants and bursaries. According to ScholarshipsCanada, more than $5 million of free money is left behind every year from scholarships and bursaries that go unclaimed.[6] These could have gone towards funding her classes or books and helped reduce the debt she graduated with.

Misstep #5: Getting No-Strings Family Support

In Canada, 43 percent of parents who expected to help their children buy their first home are at risk of delaying their own retirement and paying off debts.[7] According to a recent study in the US, that support was $39,000 on average, and if the Bank of Mom and Dad were an official business, as a whole, they'd be the seventh-biggest lender in the country.[8]

Annie's parents generously gifted her a down payment of more than $50,000 to purchase her tiny Vancouver condo so she wouldn't have to pay insurance fees (Canadian Mortgage and Housing Corporation mortgage insurance for buying with a down payment of less than 20 percent). They didn't realize that their gift could later be taken advantage of by their daughter's ex-partner.

Misstep #6: Her Parents Saved for Her, but Outside of an RESP

Annie's parents saved for her future but wanted their gift to set her up in a home early. They opened an in-trust account for her, which went to help her buy her condo.

But it would have been better for them to set funds aside in a registered education savings plan (RESP). This way, they would have earned thousands of dollars of free government money in the form of the Canada Education Savings Grant when invested in the RESP. The 20 percent savings grant that the government matches (up to a lifetime maximum) should make RESPs an irresistible option. Yet, the majority of parents (56 percent) haven't even opened up a RESP for their child.[9]

THE SOLUTION?

When it comes to love and money, the heart can cloud our minds and get us in trouble. Arming yourself with protections before, during, and after a relationship can ease the potential financial fallout. And romancing a fancy education without understanding all of your options can be a costly learning experience.

Step #1: Draft a Cohabitation Agreement Before Moving In

With more and more people opting to delay marriage, many individuals still want to share their life and expenses with a romantic partner. However, even if you rent, there's a possibility that significant other will be deemed your dependent years down the line, which could result in your financial responsibility for them if you break up.

Because Ritu claimed that she made improvements to Annie's

condo over the years and became dependent on her financial support to survive, she won a legal battle for half the equity in Annie's home, even though she never contributed a dime. Annie forced Ritu to sell the car, but they received $2,000 less than what they still owed on the loan. Because Ritu refused to uphold her end of the agreement, Annie was stuck paying out the remaining loan.

No document will protect you 100 percent of the time, but if Annie had had a clear cohabitation agreement that stated she wished to treat Ritu as a renter, not a future marriage partner, she may have been able to part with less of her hard-earned money when they split. Her agreement ideally would have spelled out that Ritu was not entitled to any share or interest in her condo, ever. It would have had a clause saying that she had the right, at any time, to ask Ritu to move out, with no financial repercussions to her. Such an agreement might have also indicated who would have ownership of items they acquired while together, such as furniture, art, and more.

Sign Here, Please!

A cohabitation agreement must be in writing and both parties need to enter into it willingly. If you're planning on cohabitating, consider investing in a lawyer who's familiar with such agreements. If you're getting married and want a similar agreement put in place, it's called a prenuptial agreement or "prenup." Note that cohabitation agreements are commonly written to apply even after marriage.

Step #2: Have the Money Talk with Your Partner Early

Why is it that we can talk about what's going on in our bedrooms but not about our finances? You may think me unromantic, but I truly believe that you can easily weave the finance conversation into a first date! You don't need to swap credit scores alongside phone numbers, but financial matters shouldn't be left out of the conversation entirely—especially if a relationship is starting to blossom.

A recent survey revealed that only 60 percent of women and 52 percent of men share their salary with their significant other.[10] Of those couples who divulged their salary details, most tended to do so only after they'd moved in together or were engaged.

If the money talk is uncomfortable for you, start slow. Try divulging some of your attitudes about finances in your stories, and then find a way to ask your love interest what money means to them. Really listen to your partner's answers, as they will provide so many clues about their financial behaviours and so much more.

For Annie, money meant security, and for Ritu, it meant freedom—but because they never had a money talk early in their relationship, they didn't realize how different they were from each other. Ritu had a propensity to spend money with a "live for today" attitude, even more so when the money wasn't earned by her. Annie was frugal and felt a sense of responsibility to provide for a loved one. And so, their two money views collided later in their relationship. An early conversation might have alerted Annie to the hidden financial cost of the relationship she was taking on.

Step #3: Keep Making Payments on All Debt Until the Dust Settles

Breaking up is hard enough to do, let alone dividing up your debts. If you have joint loans or lines of credit and your partner refuses to pay their share, keep paying the entire minimum monthly payment if possible. Once you've gone through your separation process (mediation, court, etc.), you can try to settle up then. But if you allow your joint debts to go unpaid, your credit score will suffer. Remember, credit reports don't care about what's fair or what you're owed by another person. If your name is on any debt and it's not paid, it's your financial reputation that takes the hit.

Step #4: Be Cautious When Co-Signing

As mentioned earlier, it's important to acknowledge that when you take on debt with another person (also known as co-signing), you're putting your financial life at risk. Only do this knowing that you are 100 percent responsible for the debt if your co-signer doesn't pay.

Step #5: Make Some Gifts a Loan

If you're giving a significant amount of money to a family member, it may make sense to structure it as a loan. If Annie's parents had done this, there would have been far less equity in her condo for Ritu to attack. The loan would be represented as a debt owing to her parents, not forming part of her net worth. The loan would not need to be complicated. It could be an interest-free loan with no payments, or there could be a reasonable interest rate and repayment schedule. Although something like this could be done on your own by finding an agreement with a Google search, it's probably a good idea to involve a lawyer when tens or even hundreds of thousands of dollars are at stake.

Step #6: Stay Domestic to Save on Schooling

If Annie had stayed on Canadian soil to complete her MBA, she would have saved significant dollars. The cost of a University of British Columbia MBA program is around $90,000 in Canadian dollars today; if you decided to head south for your schooling, the same degree in US dollars would be $130,500 (nearly $164,000 in Canadian dollars at the time of this writing)—not to mention the fact that she already had a condo with a manageable monthly cost, as opposed to living on campus. The bank job she ultimately got would have considered a domestic master's program as favourably as a foreign one. And most important, she would have saved tens of thousands of dollars.

Step #7: Dig into Bursaries and Grants

The best way to pay for school is with free money. Most universities have scholarships based on high school marks. For example, the University of Ottawa Admission Scholarship automatically provides between $1,000 and $4,000 to all eligible full-time students with an academic average of 80 percent or more who are studying in a direct-entry faculty or in the Faculty of Law, Civil Law Section. No application is required for this scholarship; all eligible students are automatically considered. There are lots of these scholarships available at most postsecondary schools, so be sure to do your research.

What is the difference between a scholarship and a bursary? A scholarship is awarded for academic achievements, while a bursary is awarded based on financial need. Government of Canada grants are also available to low- and middle-income students who are going to school full- or part-time. Grants can add up to thousands of dollars a year.

Cash for Learning

If you or your parents have loads of reward points, instead of trading them in for travel, there's a company that allows you to trade them in for your education—HigherEdPoints. Not all points qualify, but currently they have four participating partners: TD, CIBC, Aeroplan, and AmEx. As few as 35,000 CIBC points, for example, can equate to $250 towards your education.

If you're a mature student with RRSP assets, you can use the Lifelong Learning Plan option to take money out of your RRSP. You're able to withdraw $10,000 per calendar year (for you or your spouse). You have to pay yourself back any money taken out of your RRSP, or you face tax consequences.

Step #8: Get to Know the Benefits of RESPs

In chapter 6, we will look at the two most popular "garages," or tax shelters, in Canada. A registered education savings plan (RESP) is a third garage option. RRSPs and RESPs are tax-deferred (tax payable on withdrawal), but a TFSA is tax-free (no tax payable on withdrawal or ever). You don't get a tax deduction when you put money into an RESP, but you do get a generous government grant that's up to 20 percent of your contribution up to an annual limit, depending on your province of residence and your income. Where else can you get a 20 percent return on investment? The big plus of the RESP is that when your child withdraws from it, the proceeds are taxed in their hands, not yours.

- Individual or family plans
- Government grant up to 20%
- Withdrawals will be taxed in the hands of your child
- Grows tax-deferred
- Investments (cars) can be GICs, stocks, bonds, mutual funds, ETFs, and more

Some features of the RESP are:

- For each $2,500 you contribute per child per year, the government will match 20 percent ($500) with the Canada Education Savings Grant (CESG). If you have missed contributing in previous years, you can double up and get the 20 percent CESG grant on up to $5,000 of annual contributions. If you have a lower income, you may be able to get even more from the CESG or from the Canada Learning Bond. In some provinces, the provincial government may contribute, too.
- There's a lifetime maximum of $50,000 per child. The $50,000 limit is for all contributions for that beneficiary, even if there are multiple family members—like grandparents—who open an account. The CESG has a lifetime limit of $7,200, which you could hit by making $36,000 in contributions.
- You can set up family plans so if one of your children doesn't pursue a postsecondary education, the funds can be shared with another child.
- The plan can stay open for thirty-six years (or forty for those with disabilities), so if your child doesn't decide to go to school right away, they have time. In the event you have leftover funds in your child's RESP, you have to pay back any government grants, but the principal comes out tax-free and the investment growth can be transferred on a tax-deferred basis to your RRSP if you have RRSP room.
- You can invest in a wide range of options, such as GICs, stocks, bonds, mutual funds, ETFs, and more.

WHERE IS SHE NOW?

Annie loathed being alone, but she vowed never again to make the mistakes she had with Ritu. After their breakup, she took a one-year dating break. In month thirteen, she met Chris. It was love at first sight! This time, though, her head was going to rule, not her heart.

On their first official date, Annie laid it all on the line. She said she wanted a partner who was on the same page financially and if that scared her partner, she was okay with it. Annie was relieved when Chris shared that being fiscally responsible had been ingrained in her since she was a child. Chris totally floored Annie by sharing her credit score and net worth with her, just to make her feel more comfortable with Chris as a responsible adult. It was so refreshingly honest and kind that Annie immediately liked her even more.

Annie also decided to shift her career focus and head back to school for her PhD in psychology. It had been her real love early on, but she'd opted for an MBA because of family pressure. She knew finances would be tight while she was in school, so she was determined to find funding to support her efforts. Digging into a number of scholarships, she was able to qualify for one paying $3,000 a year and a corporate grant for $5,000. During her second year, she secured an internship at a mental health hospital that paid enough to keep her from incurring debt for her studies.

She and Chris started to live together in Chris's condo. Before Annie moved in, there was one day when Chris was acting really weird, like she was nervous.

"Just tell me," Annie said. "It's clear something's wrong."

Chris revealed that she wanted a cohabitation agreement in place to protect them both. Annie started to laugh.

"What? Why are you laughing?" Chris asked.

"Because you thought I'd say no, but I'm actually really glad you raised this."

Chris's relief was obvious, and the two sat down to hash out an equitable deal. They agreed that Annie was moving in and clearly stated that she would have no interest or share in Chris's equity, nor any future equity. Since Annie kept her place and rented it out, the agreement also stipulated that Chris was equally not entitled to any share in Annie's property or assets, and neither was obligated to provide financial support to the other for any reason now or in the future. Chris added a clause that should they part, Annie would be provided sixty days' notice to leave Chris's condo. Once they signed their agreement, they both felt like they'd succeeded at adulting in the healthiest financial ways. With the finances settled, they were free to focus on love.

Now, three years into their relationship, this couple talks about money regularly. Rather than letting finances tear them apart, it's actually the glue that keeps them together.

Working for Yourself

Renee had a great, secure job at a bank. While she loved the work and her colleagues, she decided to take the leap and start her own business as a social media consultant. She set some money aside before she quit and hoped it would be enough to start up and successfully launch her new company. But only three years into her new business, she had already blown through those savings and dug herself deep into debt for her fancy office and lifestyle.

WHERE SHE WENT WRONG

It's great to aspire to become a small business owner, but you have to do it in a financially viable way. While Renee did set some money aside, she was ill prepared for all the costs that a new business incurs, and she lacked a proper strategy and financial cushion to handle them.

Misstep #1: Miscalculating the Risks

A casualty of staring at social media feeds all day and seeing uber-successful influencers and local homegrown businesses is that it all looks so easy from afar. But becoming an entrepreneur and setting up a business is a big step that requires carefully weighing all the pros and cons and ensuring you're up for the task and all the surprises that might come along the way.

Renee's not alone in only seeing the bright side of starting a business. In 2021, Statistics Canada reported that 2.9 million Canadians are living the self-employment dream.[1] But it's wise to be aware of the dangers as well. According to data from the Bureau of Labor Statistics, as reported by Fundera, approximately 20 percent of small businesses fail within the first year.[2] By the end of the second year, 30 percent of the businesses will have failed. By the end of the fifth year, about half will have failed. And by the end of the decade, only 30 percent of the businesses will remain—a 70 percent failure rate.

Going it on your own can be incredibly rewarding and profitable. But you first need to know your temperature for risk and be totally prepared for the challenges ahead. Renee never considered the downside or financial obligations that come with opening a business, or whether she could handle the stress and time commitment—after all, her company would be entirely dependent on her. She was so preoccupied with the idea of success and wanting to prove that she could also achieve what others had, she didn't factor in these responsibilities and made a hasty decision that she would later regret.

Misstep #2: Leaving a Secure Job Too Early

When Renee quit her job, she had only $10,000 in savings and a couple of credit cards with modest limits totalling around $6,000.

But with high interest rates attached to those cards, using them should have been a last resort. She thought as soon as she opened her business, she'd be able to convince the bank to provide her with a corporate line of credit. After all, she had years of great income from her old job, a strong credit score, and minimal debt at the time. The bank, however, came back to her saying because she had zero income as a brand-new business, her venture was far too risky for them to consider. Plus, Renee's company had no credit history. This was quite a shock to hear.

As the years went on, Renee was able to get more personal credit to fund her business but never took the steps necessary to obtain and build credit in her company's name. That meant paying big bucks in interest on her credit cards and personally being on the hook for the debt she incurred to build her business.

Misstep #3: Comingling Personal and Corporate Dollars

When Renee set up her corporation, she did the right thing by getting a business bank account. It's a requirement with a separate legal entity like a corporation. The big problem was that she didn't have a credit card specifically for corporate purchases and she often mixed purchases on her cards. She didn't think it would be a big deal but when tax time came, her records were a mess. The mistakes cost her valuable time organizing everything and hundreds of dollars with her bookkeeper.

Misstep #4: Not Accounting for Lean Beginnings

Renee is a social media whiz but despises sales and marketing. She didn't realize the work and time required to get people to notice and consider a business, especially a brand-new one that no one's heard of. She thought when she opened up shop, all her years of networking would have clients banging down her door. Instead, it was more like crickets chirping each day. In a bid to make her business look more attractive, she spent money on photo shoots for her website and social media, and on furnishing her office space. When the money dried up and she only had a small list of clients that would barely cover those expenses, she considered throwing in the towel and getting a nine-to-five job again.

Misstep #5: Trying to Look Big Too Fast

Renee wanted to project a professional, successful persona and spent money ensuring she would look the part. She signed a three-year lease on a small but stylish office space. As her money dwindled, she realized how little she needed the space—after all, much of her work could be easily done online or by phone. And she didn't realize until much later the landlord could sue her personally if she broke the lease early.

She had also hired a full-time executive assistant to answer emails and phones, as she worried that personally responding might make her look too desperate or amateurish. Not only was she paying her assistant double what she was netting, she couldn't believe how much more she had to pay for her employee beyond her salary. There were costs like employer CPP (Canada Pension Plan) and EI (Employment Insurance, a federal government benefit payable if you're unable to work), Workplace Safety and Insurance Board (WSIB), vacation pay, and benefits. She didn't have any benefits herself but had to pay them to her assistant.

Renee didn't realize how long it takes to actually see a profit in a new business and instead poured money into things that wouldn't help her gain anything in the short or long term.

Misstep #6: Forgetting About Insurance and Benefits

One downside to quitting her job was losing her generous work benefit plan. Renee figured she could go without insurance for a few months, so she wouldn't have to deplete her savings on services she wouldn't even use. But she soon found herself suffering from a number of mental and physical health issues, including heightened stress from her new responsibilities and a throbbing cracked tooth. Now she felt trapped and torn between spending the little money she had left on her own health and putting it into her business.

Misstep #7: Not Setting Money Aside for Taxes

As soon as Renee opened her new business, she decided to incorporate, which cost around $2,000 up front and nearly $2,000 a year to file her corporate returns. She didn't want to be seen as a gig economy worker, but those were dollars she couldn't afford to blow.

She also saw the harmonized sales tax (HST) that she collected as her income and never set any aside. When her tax bill came each quarter and year, she never had the funds to pay it. She was forever behind with the Canada Revenue Agency (CRA), paying penalties for filing late and outsized interest for being behind. Just when she finished her payment arrangements, she owed again, and so the vicious circle continued.

Renee also made the cardinal mistake of writing off personal items, such as new outfits and family dinners, on her taxes. She may not get caught for some time or ever, but if CRA audits her, she will have to pay that money back and the compound interest.

THE SOLUTION?

Wanting to venture out on your own is a worthy aspiration that can be incredibly rewarding both personally and financially. But it's vital to plan, learn, and be honest about the risks right from the start.

Step #1: Stay Lean, Know Your Numbers

Starting a business means researching the costs and building a realistic plan for your future. Some of the most successful businesses were started in garages, basements, and kitchens. Going too big too fast means that your overhead costs could sink you before you start.

You'll want to understand the full costs before you take the entrepreneurial plunge. Determine the annual costs for an office space, staff, and other start-up costs. Figure out how much your venture will need to earn just to pay those expenses per year and whether you'll have anything left to pay yourself a salary or profit. This exercise will help you understand what you can afford.

Renee thought her years of work and excellent credit would grant her an operating line of credit to start her business. But now that she was self-employed and just starting her business, the bank only saw her as a risk and akin to having zero income. Yes, a strong credit score is important, but with no revenue, banks are very unlikely to lend to you. If you're thinking of leaving your salaried job to start a business, or for parental, family, or caregiving reasons, or to go on sabbatical, it is best to secure your lending needs while you're still employed.

Renee could have done much of her job by herself via email,

phone calls, and a good selfie stick. She didn't need to have fancy photo shoots or an assistant.

Step #2: Keep Your Day Job (for a While, Anyway)

Starting your own business can be incredibly exciting and a dream for many. But if it means jumping in when you don't have enough money saved, your venture may be doomed before it even starts.

Instead of quitting her job immediately and starting with only her limited savings, Renee could have slowly built her new business on her evenings and weekends. The salary from her bank job would have significantly reduced the pressure for her to be an instant success. This would have given her time to grow her savings and quit when she finally felt confident about the sustainability of her new business.

It's natural to want to look more successful than you are when you're starting out. But while it's nice to have a fancy office space or hire employees to off-load some work, that will leave your cash flow and margins thin or nonexistent. Ensure that all your business decisions, particularly those made early in the process, are beneficial and will not make you financially vulnerable.

Renee should have started working from home and perhaps looked into a month-to-month agreement with a shared office space to have a physical address and a place to meet clients. If she needed an assistant, she could have hired a virtual assistant instead. It would incur a hefty hourly fee compared to what she paid her full-time assistant, but she wouldn't have had all the extra costs and responsibilities of being an employer, nor would she be obligated to keep the virtual assistance during lean times.

Renee was also hasty in incorporating her business, since it cost more than she could afford. Let's look at some of the pros and cons of incorporating your business:

Pros:

- It can look more professional than a sole proprietorship.
- It's ideal if you'll have partners or are planning on selling your company one day.
- Any excess cash each year is taxed at as little as 9 to 14 percent, depending on your province of residence and other factors, which is significantly lower than personal income tax rates.
- It provides some liability protection, as the corporation is a separate legal entity from you as an individual.

Cons:

- It's costly to set up.
- Filing corporate tax returns each year is time-consuming, complex, and expensive.
- You may still be required to provide personal guarantees on money borrowed, lease agreements, and more.

Renee can dissolve her corporation if it's costing her more than it's worth. She should invest in a Chartered Professional Accountant for guidance to determine whether it's worth it for her to continue with the formal structure or move towards being a sole proprietor.

Step #3: Research Benefits and Plan for Your Own Pension

If you're an entrepreneur, you really have no one but yourself to take care of your mental and physical health, and your retirement. You can't rely on support for prescriptions or the dentist, and you don't have the padding of a pension from a company.

Planning for the Future

Here is a list of some coverage you need to consider purchasing or saving up for:

Disability insurance

This insurance pays you a monthly benefit if you're unable to work. It can be expensive, depending on what coverage you get. Be sure to read and understand the fine print to know exactly how and when you'll be eligible. For example, some policies won't pay out as long as you can perform any occupation, even if it isn't your specific one.

Disability insurance is a tax-deductible expense for a corporation, but if you need to collect on the insurance, it will be taxable to you. Alternatively, if you pay personally and go on disability, the income will be tax-free.

Critical illness insurance

In the event of a stroke, heart attack, cancer, and more, this type of insurance provides a lump-sum payment. It's tax-free and you can use the proceeds however you'd like, such as for medical treatments or for time off work. The issue with this insurance is that it gets extremely expensive as you age because your likelihood of getting one of their covered illnesses also increases with age. It is recommended that you consider this type of insurance as early as possible and look for a term-life plan where premiums don't increase as you age. Many critical illness policies have return-of-premium options at death if you never make a claim.

Keep in mind that critical illness insurance is not a replacement for disability insurance. It can complement it, but won't pay out if you can't work due to a noncritical illness.

Health and dental plans

Private plans can provide much-needed assurance and coverage if you've left your job, are self-employed, or are retiring. If you're leaving a group plan from your employer, you often have ninety days to have guaranteed acceptance into a new insurance. These plans can be pricey depending on the perks and features you choose, but most have basic coverage for dental and prescriptions; other benefits like massages, chiropractors, and therapists will likely increase the cost. Consider either buying a plan with whatever benefits you might need, or self-funding in a savings account and paying up front when the need arises.

Pension plan

As an entrepreneur or small business owner, you'll have to self-fund your retirement by saving in RRSPs and/or TFSAs. You'll also have to pay more for your own CPP as your own employer—twice as much, in fact, by paying the employee and employer contributions. If you hire a traditional employee (not a contract worker), you'll also be responsible for their employer CPP and EI contributions.

Step #4: Keep Personal and Business Accounts Separate

When you start working as a sole proprietor, you don't have to open a new bank account if you're not using a business name that differs from your own name. But it can be advantageous for record keeping. You'll need a separate account for a corporation, and try not to use your corporate account for personal expenses to simplify your bookkeeping.

If you do incorporate, you may not be able to get a corporate credit card immediately, so do your best to separate your business expenses from personal ones. This could mean using your debit card or a second personal credit card, or even getting a supplementary card on your personal account. Just be sure to only use one card for all business purchases. That way, when you receive your credit card statement, you won't have a confusing mix of purchases and have to waste time sorting everything out. At tax time, these neatly organized statements will make your bookkeeping that much easier.

Step #5: Set Enough Aside for Tax Time

When you're a salaried employee, your company will withhold taxes from your paycheques and submit them to the government on your behalf, so you shouldn't owe anything at tax time.

But if you're self-employed, you're 100 percent responsible for reporting your income accurately, setting those taxes aside, and paying those yourself. Unfortunately, many entrepreneurs struggle their first few years financially. It's so tempting to only see and budget with your pre-tax dollars, or to collect HST/GST and use that money instead of putting it in reserve and paying CRA every quarter. You'll want to avoid this at all costs, as this is tax avoidance and a criminal offence. CRA can be reasonable in setting up payment plans if you get behind in your taxes, but it also has the power to garnish your pay, contact your clients and get promised payments sent straight to it, seize your home, and so much more.

To avoid this, train your mind to see gross dollars for what they are. Estimate what you think you'll earn and figure out how much tax owing that will represent. Every time you're paid, set that percentage aside in a separate bank account. Call that your "tax owing" account. If your company or side hustle earns (or is expected to earn) more than $30,000 a year, you'll typically have to charge GST or HST. Each province has different rules and amounts for their sales taxes, which currently range from 5 percent to 13 percent. You'll then want to open a second bank account for your GST/HST and religiously set that aside. Many entrepreneurs are tempted to use these dollars collected on behalf of the government when they're in a bind, but don't be lured. There are hefty penalties for not paying your GST/HST, and unlike back taxes owed (personal or corporate), CRA is less inclined to offer payment plans for GST/HST owing. Plus, there's high interest accruing on balances as well. So, make sure to stay up-to-date on your remittances and instalments to CRA.

To recap, your new venture should have three bank accounts:

- An operating account
- A no-fee HST/GST account
- A no-fee tax account

If you choose the path of the entrepreneur, you'll have to budget for:

- Personal income tax on your business's earnings minus legitimate business expenses

- Corporate tax on the corporation's net earnings that year, plus any money you have left in the corporation at the end of each fiscal year
- Contributions to the Canada Pension Plan for yourself and any employees
- Contributions to voluntary Employment Insurance for you and mandatory EI for employees (most often, those who are self-employed are generally unable to collect on benefits, so do your research before opting in for voluntary contributions)
- GST, HST, and other sales tax obligations, depending on the province in which you conduct business

Step #6: Learn the Tax Rules

Starting a new business can be a complex and confusing process. When Renee had questions about what expenses could be written off for business purposes, she should have consulted a tax preparer or a Chartered Professional Accountant. This would have mitigated the risk of being audited by CRA and being forced to pay back compound interest on any erroneous claims. It also would have helped her navigate any other tricky financial obligations she didn't fully understand.

Financial professionals can help you avoid leaving free money on the table. For example, if you're self-employed and use your home to conduct your business, you can claim a portion of your mortgage interest, property taxes, utilities, and more. Tax rules are often changing, and having a professional on your side is a great way to ensure that you stay on top of your responsibilities and don't have to pay for it later. And the great news is that their fees are tax deductible if you are incorporated.

WHERE IS SHE NOW?

Renee learned the hard way that in business, cash is king! She wouldn't give up on her dream, but she did have to take a step back.

Her aunt was a highly successful businesswoman and a retired Chartered Professional Accountant. Renee met with her several times for some free advice. Renee's aunt suggested that she make the toughest decision of an entrepreneur's life—wind things down for now and start again stronger with many lessons learned.

It wasn't a free ticket out of trouble, though. She had to negotiate her way out of an office lease and let go of her assistant. Laying her assistant off with severance and knowing she had a few months of EI to collect eased the pain a bit for them both. And at her aunt's suggestion, Renee worked to dissolve her corporation. The lessons were hard and financially painful, but shutting down was the right financial move.

Renee kept in contact with her old boss and co-workers at the bank. She asked for her old job back and was given a similar one where she could work remotely most of the time. This worked perfect for her long-term plan. She could work from home and use her evenings and weekends to slowly reframe her next business.

It was tough working a nine-to-five job again, but she was grateful for the steady income. She hustled for new clients on the side, too, and it felt like she was attracting just the right accounts at the right pace.

In less than two years, Renee saved enough to pay off all of the debt she incurred from her first failed business. She also amassed a robust personal emergency account. She worked with her business banker to secure a $25,000 personal line of credit, which was easy with her full-time salary and the cash flow from her side income.

She still didn't qualify for any business credit, but having the line of credit while she didn't actually need it provided comfort.

She's not entirely sure when she'll fully go back into business. For now, she's dropped to part-time at the bank, freeing up some of her schedule for more clients. She loves that she's now able to work entirely from home, is incurring minimal staff costs, and has her finances in order. But what she enjoys most of all is knowing she doesn't owe CRA or anyone money.

Renee added up how much interest she was paying on her back taxes and for her high-interest-rate credit cards. It was a whopping $300 a month at times. She currently invests that amount monthly. For now, things are going great. Renee enjoys taking one slow and steady step at a time towards her entrepreneurship dream.

6

Self-Worth = Net Worth

Eloise had a banner year back in 2007. She had a solid income and all of her debts paid off except for her mortgage. She found herself with a juicy bonus of $20,000 from her company at the end of the year. She threw it all into the stock market, plus she invested $50,000 she had in savings and took out an RRSP loan for $30,000, making her total stock market investments a whopping $100,000. Sounds good, right?

Well, it was . . . for a while. But then her investments started to plummet and she began to panic. It was 2008, and the financial crisis hit hard. Eloise's investments tanked. She was horrified to watch her money drop 5 percent, then 10 percent, and when it kept plummeting to a 25 percent loss, she couldn't take the pain any longer. She sold her investments at a huge loss and vowed never to play the stock market again.

WHERE SHE WENT WRONG

Eloise isn't alone in making the mistake of jumping in and out of the stock market at the wrong times. Let's have a look at her missteps to learn from them.

First off, Eloise failed to ask the advice of a financial professional to help her accurately assess her ability to handle risk and analyze the right mix of investments for her situation. She hadn't diversified her investments, either, which left her vulnerable when the markets took a hit. She thought she was saving money by making decisions all on her own, but sadly, she learned the hard way that sometimes seeking the advice of experts really does pay off in the end.

Misstep #1: Not Understanding Asset Classes

You've heard the sage advice of not putting all of your eggs in one basket, right? Asset classes are different baskets of investments. Some baskets (investment classes) are super risky and offer the opportunity for a greater return in the long term. Some are ultra safe but don't pay much because of low interest rates. There are all kinds of asset classes and options that we'll examine shortly.

One asset class that Eloise invested in heavily was stocks, because she was under the false impression that RRSPs don't really earn much. She didn't realize that in her high-income tax bracket, she was leaving juicy tax deductions on the table each year by not maxing out her RRSPs. She's not alone. Many Canadians don't realize that an RRSP isn't an investment—it's a tax shelter. Eloise went straight to the stock market when she actually could have embraced a lot of savings first at a lower risk level or balanced her portfolio with less risky alternatives. If she still invested in stocks but did so in an RRSP, she would have received a sizable tax deduction.

Misstep #2: Thinking the Past Repeats Itself

Eloise's family made a lot of money in stocks in the eighties and nineties. She assumed that past performance meant future success, so she followed their strategy. Unfortunately, past performance provides zero guarantee of future returns in any asset class. Plus, in our rapidly changing world, industries can disappear almost overnight. Companies that were once behemoths crumble while new ones rise from the ashes, and if you're invested in one of the former, you can see your money disappear. Eloise thought there was predictability in her choices, but in fact, she needed more of a foundation in how to select the right range of investments so that her money could grow over the long term.

Misstep #3: Failing to Mitigate Risk with Diversification and Trying to Time the Market

It's been said that an investment portfolio is like a bar of soap: the more you touch it, the smaller it gets. Like many investors, Eloise was sure she could weather the ups and downs of a turbulent market, but she wasn't prepared for just how volatile it can be.

Eloise also mistakenly thought she could time the market—pick the lows and highs—which is impossible for even the most seasoned financial professional. She didn't understand that while investing heavily in stocks magnified her potential returns, it also exposed her to more risk than she could realistically handle. When stock markets are roaring, it's human nature to want to get in on the action. But that's precisely when investors need to really understand the potential downside and how to invest with a balanced approach.

Eloise's lack of diversification meant that her entire portfolio was going either up or down. Riding the highs is fun, but if you sell when the markets drop, it might have been better never to have invested in the first place. When markets drop, it's only a loss on paper. But if you sell, you actualize that loss. Eloise didn't have to sell at the low point. In fact, if she hadn't panicked and had instead held on, she could have made all her money back and much more in just a few years.

Because of her bad experiences in 2008, Eloise is now worried about putting her money in any market. She's been sitting on her savings, waiting out market highs and lows. Her failure to act has meant she's lost tens of thousands of dollars over the past decade or so.

THE SOLUTION?

When the COVID-19 pandemic hit the world in March 2020, stock markets began to plummet. The news was calling this crash the worst since the Great Depression. My inbox was exploding with investors wondering if they should sell or wait things out. Many people sold low, only to lose out when the market swung upwards later in the year. When it comes to investments, patience is a virtue, and timing is everything. Let's have a look at how Eloise could have done things differently in the past and how she can still make positive investment decisions going forwards. We'll also review some terminology that will help us get investment savvy.

Step #1: Understand Asset Classes

When it comes to spreading out your risk with investments, the financial industry looks to three main asset classes. These are cash, bonds (also known as fixed income), and stocks (also called equity). There are, of course, other classes, such as real estate, precious metals, and more, but the first three are the building blocks with which to diversify investments. Each asset class carries its own risk and return potential.

Cash investments

This can be cash in your bank account or a short-term investment such as a government treasury bill or term deposit. These are liquid investments that you can sell immediately or within a few months to less than a year. They're considered very safe, and generally, you won't lose what you invest. Cash investments are savings accounts, T-bills (short-term, safe, and liquid government offerings), money market mutual funds, and cash on hand.

The problem with the cash asset class right now is that interest rates are extremely low. After you receive your interest, factor in the tax you'll have to pay on it and inflation (the increased costs of things), and you likely aren't earning much at all.

If you hold the cash assets outside of a tax shelter (called a non-registered account), then you pay tax on the interest earned each year or when you sell them. Most people will pay 15 to more than 50 percent on the interest earned. However, if you have your cash assets in a tax shelter like an RRSP or TFSA, you don't pay tax on what your funds earn.

Bonds/fixed-income investments

A bond is a debt owed to you by a government, province, municipality, or corporation. When governments need to raise money from investors, they offer a bond. You lend them an amount for a period of time, and, depending on how secure they are, you're offered an interest payment (called the yield) in exchange for lending them your money. This class is often called "fixed income" because you know exactly how much interest you'll be paid and can receive that interest as monthly, quarterly, or annual income payments. You can also elect to not receive payments at all and allow the interest to compound (earn interest on your interest).

A bond from the Government of Canada, for example, is much safer than one from your province or city but also offers lower interest. Bonds can be bought and sold on a bond market and tend to have long maturities of ten, twenty, or even thirty years. You can sell your bonds before their maturity, but if you do so, you may be selling them at a loss.

This class can also include a guaranteed investment certificate (GIC) from your bank. With GICs, you lend your bank money for one to five years and they offer you a rate of interest in exchange. Like with the cash class, interest rates are very low, but your principal amount invested is guaranteed at maturity. If you invest $10,000, you'll receive your $10,000 back plus interest each year, which can compound if you don't take it out. Unlike bonds, you cannot sell your GIC before its maturity date (unless you purchase a redeemable GIC, which has a lower interest rate than a non-redeemable GIC).

GICs, bonds, and other types of fixed income are generally taxed at the same rate as interest in a savings account—ranging from 15 percent to more than 50 percent depending on income level and where you live. There are other types of fixed income, like preferred shares, that may pay dividends instead of interest and be subject to a lower tax rate.

If you receive $100 interest on your GIC, bond, or bank account, you will have to claim that interest as income and will be fully taxed on it. Depending on your marginal tax bracket (how much tax you pay federally and provincially), your profit may be reduced.

Stocks/equity

A stock is an investment in a company that allows you to share in their ups and downs. Instead of lending money to the company, as with a bond, you own a part of that company, referred to as equity. Depending on the type of shares you own, you may or may not be able to also vote on major company decisions; common shares have voting rights, while preferred shares do not.

This class of investments can be moderately to super risky. You can invest in blue-chip stocks that pay high dividends and may be less volatile than some other stocks. There are more junior companies that can provide great promise of future returns but can also be more volatile.

When you own stocks, there are different ways your income gets taxed. You can receive a dividend that is taxable in the year you receive it. Canadian dividends benefit from special tax treatment and are therefore taxable at a lower rate than interest income. For example, if someone has $75,000 of income and earns an extra dollar of Canadian dividends, the tax they'd pay on that extra dollar would be between 8 and 21 percent, depending on where they live. If it was an extra dollar on interest income (or foreign dividends, salary, or other income, for that matter), they'd pay 28 to 38 percent tax instead. Foreign dividends are taxed at the same rate as interest and don't get the special Canadian dividend tax treatment.

You can also earn a capital gain (or loss) when you own a stock. When you sell a stock for a profit, 50 percent of the gain is taxable as a capital gain. Half the gain is tax-free. Stocks generally earn higher rates of return than bonds over the long term, despite the short-run volatility.

Balancing Act

A word of caution when investing in stocks or bonds: because you can lose some or all of your money in a single stock, you need to invest in a diversified portfolio of stocks and understand the risk and what you're buying. Take some time to educate yourself and ease into equity-type investments. At the same time, don't let fear settle you into only investing in safe investments like bonds and cash equivalents. Remember: balance is key.

Eloise didn't fully understand the market, nor did she diversify to weather the ups and downs. If she'd had a balanced portfolio of stocks, bonds, and cash, she wouldn't have experienced the extreme dips to her investments and thus, she likely wouldn't have panicked and sold at the wrong time.

Step #2: Learn How Inflation Erodes Your Wealth

Inflation is the future buying power on your money today. If you've ever heard an elder lament that they could buy a coffee for fifty cents when they were young, whereas a coffee can now cost more than five dollars, you've received a lesson on inflation. As you know, the price of many things increases each year. The inflation rate is measured by the CPI—the consumer price index. As inflation increases, you have to earn more on your money to keep up with it. Inflation and interest rates typically work in tandem. Currently, the inflation rate is around 2 percent. To keep pace with how much more things will cost at the end of the year, you'd need to earn at least 2 percent more to have the equivalent buying power you had the year before.

To give you an idea of inflation rates by year:

- 2019: 1.95 percent
- 2018: 2.27 percent
- 2017: 1.60 percent
- 2016: 1.43 percent

If the economy heats up quickly and people are willing to pay more for goods and services, inflation can increase. When that happens, the Bank of Canada tries to ensure that spending and consumer debt don't get out of hand. This is done by increasing interest rates. As interest rates go up, borrowing becomes more expensive. That means it becomes more costly to borrow to buy a car, a home, or furniture, or go on vacation, which will naturally slow down people's spending.

As a point of reference, the average inflation rate in Canada in the 1980s was 10.11 percent.[1] And for that decade, mortgage rates were anywhere from 14 to 18 percent. That meant it was considerably more expensive to pay the mortgage on a home. As you can imagine, those high rates made it much more difficult to get approved for a mortgage and thus affected the values of homes because fewer people could afford them.

After losing so much in the market in 2008 and 2009, Eloise had left her money in a regular savings account earning less than 1 percent interest per year. After she subtracts inflation and the tax she'll have to pay on that tiny 1 percent rate of return, while it's not obvious, her so-called savings are actually costing her.

Step #3: Get to Know the Power of Compound Interest

To illustrate the awesome powers of compound interest, allow me to propose an offer to you. Would you prefer a million dollars right now or a penny that doubled every day for thirty days? Which one would you choose?

Let's see how that penny makes out in a month of doubling each day:

Day 1: 1 cent
Day 3: 4 cents
Day 7: 64 cents

Pretty paltry so far, right? Bet you wish you chose the million-dollar option.

Day 9: $2.56
Day 11: $10.24

Now things are getting a little interesting.

Day 13: $40.96
Day 15: $163.84
Day 18: $1,310.72

Wow, a couple of weeks in and it's at four digits already. Are you surprised?

Day 19:	$2,621.44
Day 23:	$41,943.04
Day 27:	$671,088.64
Day 30:	$5,368,709.12

Unfortunately, there's no such thing as a magical doubling penny, but I hope the above illustrates the miraculous power of compounding. Our intuition says, of course, a million dollars now must be more profitable than the doubling penny. But the numbers don't lie.

If Eloise took advantage of compound interest and the tax deductions of an RRSP, for example, and the tax deferral from the shelter, compounding would look even more magical. Because she doesn't pay tax each year on what her investments earn (or when they're sold), that money could keep earning income and growing on itself. When you're saving for your future, it takes a long time to see the effect of compounding, as with the doubling penny, but once that snowball gains some traction and you roll it downhill, the result is thrilling.

Let's look at a more realistic example of how compounding can benefit your investments: How does compound interest look investing $10,000 for twenty years (with no new deposits) at a 6 percent annual rate of return reinvested each year?

Year 1:	$10,000 plus $600	= $10,600.00
Year 5:	$12,624.76 plus $757.49	= $13,382.25
Year 10:	$16,894.76 plus $1,013.70	= $17,908.46
Year 15:	$22,608.99 plus $1,356.56	= $23,965.55
Year 20:	$30,255.93 plus $1,815.35	= $32,071.28

I don't know about you, but seeing those numbers makes me feel excited. As you witness the compounding build slowly at first but gain significant momentum after the first ten years, you can't help but see how compounding can work for you. You'll see at year fifteen, your $10,000 has more than doubled, and by year twenty, it's increased threefold from day one. Earning an extra $13,965.55 took a long fifteen years. But look how fast the remaining five years earned $8,105.73. Time and patience make compounding exhilarating!

Compounding in a tax-deferred or tax-free account like an RRSP or TFSA can be very exciting, too. In a non-registered account, taxes reduce your ability to compound your investments because you'll always be paying some of the income or growth to the government. If you have a group RRSP or pension at work with a matching contribution from your employer, compounding can be even more impactful.

Step #4: Know What "the Markets" Are Before You "Play" Them

When you hear the news reports about how the "markets" are doing, they're referring to the stock markets as a whole entity. Let's look at some of the major North American indexes, which are lists of businesses from which you can buy and sell stock. A company can be listed on more than one index or "exchange."

Canada

S&P/TSX

The S&P/TSX Composite Index is the main stock market in Canada. It's the benchmark (standard point of reference) Canadian index that represents approximately 70 percent of the total market capitalization of the Toronto Stock Exchange. About 250 companies are included in the index.

If investing in the stock market is right for you, you might consider investing in an index as a whole, as opposed to buying some of the individual stocks on your own, to get exposure to a vast number of industries from banking to energy to gold, entertainment, and so much more.

United States

Dow

The Dow Jones Industrial Average (a.k.a. the Dow or Dow Jones) is a stock market index that measures the performance of thirty large companies listed on stock exchanges in the US. The Dow, a very narrow representation of the US stock market, includes companies such as Apple and American Express.

Nasdaq

The Nasdaq Composite Index is an index of more than 2,500 stocks listed on the Nasdaq exchange, which includes the world's foremost technology and biotech giants, such as Google, Microsoft, Oracle, Amazon, and Intel.

S&P 500

The S&P 500, or simply the S&P, is a stock market index that measures the performance of five hundred large companies listed on stock exchanges in the United States. It is one of the most commonly followed equity indexes. Companies listed include Bank of America, Chevron, Dollar Tree, Domino's Pizza, and Johnson & Johnson.

If all of this is making your head spin, that's okay. The markets are to be respected and understood before jumping in. But also realize that by staying too safe in today's low-interest-rate environment, your money will never make much money. Take time to educate yourself; ease in with low, regular monthly contributions when you're ready; and search for a good financial professional to provide guidance. If you're a seasoned investor with years of experience to weather the ups and downs of the markets, then you're likely well versed enough to truly protect against the risk of investing in equities.

Step #5: Recognize the Difference Between Mutual Funds and ETFs

Now that you understand how individual investments work for you and you're ready to invest, you may wonder where to start. If you have loads of money to invest, there are lots of low-cost strategies that exist with wealth management firms and portfolio managers. But most Canadians are starting with modest savings. Unfortunately, the Canadian financial industry is geared towards the wealthy. Many portfolio managers won't consider working with a client unless they have a half million dollars or more to invest. There are advisors at your bank and independent ones who will work with investors who are just starting out, but those clients are likely to receive limited advice.

Whether you're working with an advisor or a portfolio manager, one of the most important things to know is what fees you're paying—hidden or otherwise—for financial products.

Mutual funds

Let's say you have $10,000 to invest and want to save $100 a month. If you were trying to buy some stocks and bonds, it could be tricky to build a diversified portfolio. The transaction costs to buy a bunch of different investments could add up, let alone the work involved to pick all the investments.

In come mutual funds. What if you wanted to buy a variety of bank stocks and shares in the energy sector, have some gold and silver exposure, and maybe purchase a few government bonds to add some stability to your stock exposure? That's where a mutual fund could be a brilliant solution for you. You could buy one Canadian Equity mutual fund (that has a number of bank and other stocks within it), put some money into a precious metals fund (that invests in gold, sliver, and more), and invest in a bond fund that has dozens of different bonds within it.

Buying Individual Securities	*Investing in a Mutual or Pooled Fund*
Need a large investment to spread out your risk.	Can start investing in some funds with as little as $500 or $25 a month.
There are costs to buy and sell the securities.	Embedded costs within the fund to buy and sell investments on your behalf (instead of you making the trades yourself).
You need to choose what you'll buy, when to buy, and when to sell (or have an advisor who will do this for you).	The mutual manager buys and sells on your behalf—you don't have to make decisions on what securities are bought or sold.

Buying Individual Securities	*Investing in a Mutual or Pooled Fund*
You can't necessarily sell your investment on any given day—there has to be a buyer for what you're selling.	You can sell your mutual fund units on any business day. (When you invest in a stock, you receive "shares." In a mutual fund, you receive "units.")
You have to do your own research or find an advisor who is knowledgeable to help you make key buy-and-sell decisions.	Mutual funds buy and sell on your behalf. If you buy a Canadian Equity mutual fund that has sixty stocks in it, for example, the mutual fund manager will be doing the research and buying and selling on your behalf.

The biggest drawback of mutual funds is that many have high management fees—called a management expense ratio, or MER—for actively managed funds. Canada has some of the highest fund fees in the world.

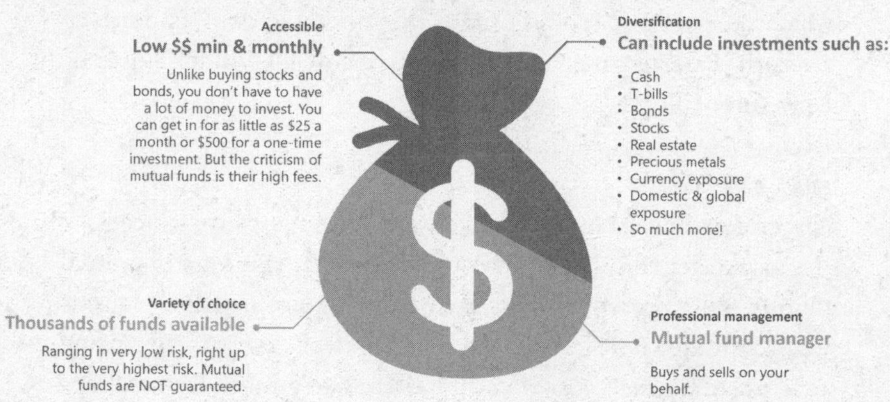

Actively managed funds

These funds have a mutual fund manager choosing stocks, bonds, and other securities (depending on the type of mutual fund) on the fund's behalf. They're using their research and discretion as to what to buy, sell, or hold. This service comes at a cost, and it's argued that a mutual manager can rarely beat what the market does itself, especially after fees. And even if they can beat the market one year, they may not do so the next year. It can be really tough to consistently beat the market (after fees) over a long period of time.

Passively managed funds

These are funds that you can still get into for a low investment amount and/or monthly investment. But in these, there's no manager actively choosing what to buy or sell. They're simply mirroring what an index does. An index is a grouping of securities like the TSX—the largest and most actively traded stocks in Canada. You can buy a bond index, precious metals index, energy index, and so much more. There's no "person" making decisions. You're simply buying the market or sector as a whole. Because there isn't a person making those active decisions, the fees tend to be much lower, which means these types of funds don't need to earn as much of a return. Passively managed funds are also called index funds or ETFs (more on this below).

Target-date funds

Target-date mutual funds gradually and automatically reduce your risk as you get closer and closer to retirement. This kind of mutual fund is often presented in defined contribution pension plans as well as group RRSPs. They take the guesswork out of rebalancing your portfolio each year if you'd like to take a more backseat approach to your investments. Each year as you get closer to retirement, you should be adjusting your investment mix based on your unique situation. But generally speaking, as you near retirement (five or ten years before), you likely need to reduce your equity exposure. Instead of doing this on your own or with your advisor, you can simply purchase target-date funds that will do this for you. You choose your desired retirement year, and your risk is gradually reduced as you near that date.

ETFs

Exchange-traded funds have exploded in popularity because of their low fees and ease of buying. Like a mutual fund, an ETF can be bought or sold on any business day. ETFs mirror the underlying indexes they represent (US stock market, global bond market, technology sector, etc.). They can be broad (North American stock markets) or very narrowly focused (cyber solutions or social media tech giants). ETFs are similar to index mutual funds but tend to have even lower fees. They also trade like stocks on a stock exchange that you can buy during the trading day, compared to mutual funds, which are valued once at the end of the day.

MERs

"Management expense ratio" (MER) refers to the fees you pay for the management of a mutual fund. The more active management you have (i.e., a mutual fund manager choosing the types of investments in the fund), the more you'll pay. If the manager is simply buying in accordance with what the market is doing (such as with an index fund or an ETF), the fees are far lower. A higher MER means that you will receive less money from your investments, as the fee will be deducted from whatever money the fund makes. This can become especially costly if the market is down, as you'll be dealing with both a loss in your investments and a management fee.

If you invested $500 a month for twenty years at a 6 percent return, let's see what you would have in your pocket if you bought a mutual fund on your own, bought a mutual fund within your group employer plan, or bought an ETF:

- With the mutual fund, you'd have somewhere between $158,499.57 and $178,501.21.
- With the group plan mutual fund, you'd have $189,583.12 and $214,183.04.
- With the ETF, you'd have, on average, $219,254.91.

Here's what you can expect to pay for each scenario:

- The average mutual fund has an MER of 2 percent but can range up to 3 percent or more.[2]
- The average mutual fund within your employer group RRSP or TFSA plan will likely have an average MER of 0.5 to 1.5 percent for similar investments, but it depends on the plan.

- Some of the largest, simplest ETFs charge fees as low as 0.05 percent and are 0.31 percent on average.

When your investments are doing well, you want to keep as much in your pocket as possible. And when markets drop, you don't want big fees adding to your losses. From the example above, we can see that between the average ETF and the most expensive mutual fund, you're looking at a difference of $60,821.34 just in fees alone. It's important that you pay attention to all fees—MERs but also commissions and any others—so you can earn substantially more in the long term.

Non-sheltered (registered) investments

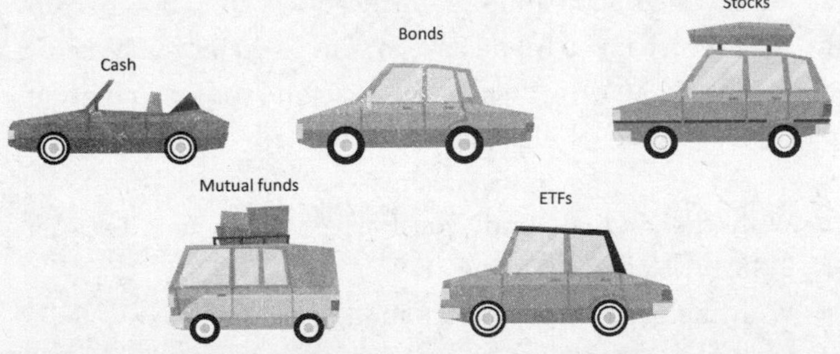

If your "cars" (investments) are hanging out on the street (no shelter), they get taxed each year on the interest they earn, or growth when you sell them. Investments without a shelter are called NON-REGISTERED ACCOUNTS

Before we dig into tax shelters in the next step, above are the basic types of investments ("cars") you can turn to for growing your wealth. If your cars are sitting on the street (without a shelter), they're subject to tax (either each year or when you sell them). If you have investments outside of a shelter, they're called non-registered accounts. Now let's look at the benefits you'll get by putting these investments in one or more shelters.

Step #6: Get Familiar with Tax Shelters

There are two main tax shelters in Canada and both are often misunderstood.

The first is an RRSP (registered retirement savings plan) and the other is a TFSA (tax-free savings account). I wish the government had named the TFSA differently, because the words "savings account" lead many to think the TFSA is simply a low-interest savings account. It can be, but it's also so much more!

Think of the RRSP and TFSA as empty garages. That's what a tax shelter is. You have to put "cars" (investments) into them, and depending on the rules of the tax shelter, there are differing perks and penalties. The cars that you park in your RRSP or TFSA garage can be identical or quite different. Both allow you a plethora of options, from GICs and savings accounts to stocks, bonds, mutual funds, ETFs, and more. The only difference is the tax treatment.

Here's a comparison between the two:

Registered Retirement Savings Plan

- When you put money into this shelter, you receive a tax deduction that is based on your marginal tax bracket. The higher your tax bracket, the higher the deduction.
- Your money grows tax-deferred, meaning you only pay tax when you take the money out of the shelter.
- If you don't use your "contribution room" in a given year, it carries forwards indefinitely.
- If you take money out of your RRSP, you don't get that RRSP room back the next year.
- If you aren't part of a pension plan, you're allowed to contribute 18 percent of your previous year's earned income per year. In 2021, the maximum RRSP limit for the year was $27,830. To find out how much you're able to contribute to your RRSP, check your notice of assessment (the blue forms you receive in the mail) from CRA or head online to set up or check your tax account.
- If you take money out, the government will withhold tax from your withdrawal. That means a $1,000 withdrawal won't leave you with $1,000 in your hands. You also will have to include the amount you took out on your taxes the next year, so depending on your income, you may end up having to pay more tax.

- Your investments grow tax-deferred
- You receive a tax deduction when investing
- You're taxed when you take your money out
- First-time Home Buyers' Plan provision
- Lifelong Learning Plan provision

Tax-Free Savings Account

- You don't receive a tax deduction.
- You don't pay tax on any interest, dividends, or capital gains you earn within the TFSA.
- Any withdrawals you make in a year increase your TFSA room the next year.
- The 2021 contribution limit was $6,000. If you never contributed, that "room" waits around for you when you can. If you were eighteen years old or older in 2009, when TFSAs were created, your available limit as of 2021 is $75,500.
- If you don't use your "contribution room" in a given year, it carries forwards indefinitely.
- You can take out money from a TFSA at any time without a tax penalty.

- Your investments grow tax-free
- No tax deduction
- No tax when you take your money out
- You can put withdrawals back the following year

There are two provisions for taking your money out of an RRSP without a tax penalty—the Home Buyers' Plan (HBP), for first-time home buyers, and the Lifelong Learning Plan (LLP). With the HBP, you can take out up to $35,000 from your RRSP to buy your first home. You have to pay any withdrawals back to yourself within fifteen years, but there's a two-year grace period after withdrawals, so you don't have to start paybacks right away (some restrictions apply). With the LLP, you can take out up to $10,000 in a given year and $20,000 in total. You must repay the entire amount within ten years and you have to pay at least one-tenth of your withdrawal each year. You can use your LLP for yourself or your common-law partner/spouse.

I hope you can see how powerful these two tax shelters are! If Eloise had known about the advantages of both, she may have made different investment decisions—ones that would have left her with tax savings and less risk overall.

Where Should I Invest?

As we already covered, different investments are taxed more preferentially than others (equities and Canadian dividends). That means if you've maxed out your RRSP and TFSA, and you still have cars sitting on the road (non-registered accounts), you'll want to make sure that your most tax-efficient investments (stocks and dividends) are on the road and the least tax-efficient (cash, bonds, and investments that produce interest income) are sheltered in your RRSP and TFSA when possible.

If you can say yes to the following, an RRSP may be right for you:

- Are you in a high tax bracket, meaning you pay a high rate of income tax?
- Can you assuredly invest this money and not access it until retirement?
- Do you have enough emergency savings to avoid dipping into your RRSPs before retirement?
- Are you free of debt from high-interest-rate credit cards?

If you're mostly agreeing with the following, a TFSA may be better suited to you:

- I'm in a low marginal tax bracket.
- I'm unsure whether I can leave my money untouched until retirement.

- I'm looking for a place to build my emergency savings.
- I've maxed out my RRSP contributions.
- I have a pension at work and therefore can't contribute a lot to RRSPs (because the pension uses up some or all of my RRSP room for a given year).

Step #7: Dig into Diversification and Realize Your Risk and the Importance of Rebalancing

Harry Markowitz won a Nobel Prize in economics in the 1990s for developing a model to help investors determine their ideal amount of risk and their potential return based on the number of years invested and the risk level. The model is called the efficient frontier (EF).

Simply put, if you're invested in a low-risk asset, your expected return should be low. Medium- and high-risk investments come with the expectation of a higher return. But no matter how much risk you take, at some point, you shouldn't expect any further return.

The EF suggests lowering your risk by introducing assets that might increase it. For example, if you only invested in lower-risk bonds, by introducing some equities into your portfolio, you can actually decrease your overall risk. Why? Because when bonds go down, stocks often go up. This is called negative correlation and it can be protective, leaving you to sleep more soundly at night.

If you own stocks or bonds, it might be wise to invest in some that zig when the others zag. And it's always a good idea to rebalance your investments every year, or even more frequently if markets are volatile. If you're working with an advisor, they'll often contact you annually to do so. If it's a mutual fund, the fund manager will balance your funds yearly. If you're using a robo-advisor, they'll often automatically rebalance your portfolio frequently as well.

Your advisor should ask you questions to help evaluate your risk tolerance and determine the right mix of investments to suit your situation. Questions might include:

- What is your time horizon for these investments?
- How much of a drop (if any) can you tolerate when it comes to your investments?
- Do you consider yourself an experienced investor?

The advisor will help you determine your ideal diversification of assets, helping you avoid putting all your eggs in one basket. Below is a common distribution for an investor with a moderate risk tolerance and long-term time horizon:

- 10 percent: cash
- 30 percent: bonds or fixed income
- 60 percent: stocks or equities

Let's say that after a year of having this allocation of investments, the stock market significantly increased and your equity investments jumped substantially in value, but your bonds and cash didn't perform as well. Now your portfolio is skewed from the original recommended mix determined by your risk profile, which could look something like this:

- 8 percent: cash
- 20 percent: bonds or fixed income
- 72 percent: stocks or equities

If you're working with a financial advisor, they'll suggest rebalancing your portfolio each year to get it back to an ideal percentage split. If you're a DIY investor, you'll want to make this adjustment on your own frequently. Just be sure to rebalance while keeping in mind your ability to handle risk and volatility. In the non-rebalanced scenario, for example, the higher allocation to equities might be considered too risky—in that case, it might be worth sticking to the original percentages, otherwise known as rebalancing.

Step #8: Time the Market Using Dollar-Cost Averaging

Dollar-cost averaging is a prudent strategy that smooths out the ups and downs, regardless of whether you're getting in or out of the market.

To illustrate the seesaw market moves of the S&P/TSX Composite Index, looking at it over a year (February 21, 2020, to February 19, 2021), you'll see a high followed by a significant low, and then a crescendo to a new high:

- The high was 17,843.53 on February 21, 2020 (right before the COVID crisis hit).
- The low was 11,851.81 on March 20, 2020 (when the height of the COVID fears were felt).
- A new high of 18,384.27 was reached on February 19, 2021.

With so many businesses shuttering and everyone being asked to stay home, how many people would have thought that it would be the ideal time to invest? And yet, March 20 was actually a great day to invest—easy to spot in hindsight but impossible to predict at the time.

Many professionals suggest that, instead of trying to pick the right day to invest, you should choose one day a month to automatically invest a certain amount of money, regardless of the markets' performance.

Let's look back over the twelve-month window I just mentioned and see how dollar-cost averaging would have played out on the

S&P/TSX Composite Index. Let's assume the investment happens on first of the month. (In the case of holidays and weekends falling on the first, the next immediate business day was used.) Each number represents the value of the S&P/TSX on that given day.

- March 2, 2020: 16,553.26
- April 1, 2020: 12,876.37
- May 4, 2020: 14,745.04
- June 1, 2020: 15,236.21
- July 2, 2020: 15,622.40
- August 4, 2020: 16,368.03
- September 1, 2020: 16,644.99
- October 1, 2020: 16,184.54
- November 2, 2020: 15,696.87
- December 1, 2020: 17,296.93
- January 4, 2021: 17,527.77
- February 1, 2021: 17,692.45

Think of the S&P/TSX value on any given day as a share price on a particular stock. But it's actually a basket of them. To figure out what the average price was in the example above, you would add them all up, divide by twelve, and see that average was 16,037.07. But you'll also notice the lowest price in the example was on April 1. You've heard about buying low and selling high, right? Well, we've already discussed how it's impossible even for the professionals to forecast when to do that.

By picking a day each month and sticking to investing that day no matter if the market is high or low, you will average out a buy-in price that smooths out the ups and downs. Sure, if you had a crystal ball, you could have bought in at the low in my example and sold near the height and made a nearly 40 percent gain. But knowing that is unrealistic, so the next best option is dollar-cost averaging: forcing yourself to buy consistently knowing some months the index will be more expensive, and some months the index will be on sale.

WHERE IS SHE NOW?

Eloise reached out to her job's HR department to dig into her group RRSP and better understand her pension. She found out that she was forgoing more than $1,200 a year in matching incentives with the RRSP, not to mention the tax deduction. She met with the plan provider, who had her move her group RRSP funds from cash slowly to a fifteen-year target-date fund within the plan. She feels comfortable that they're rebalancing her investments and slowly reducing her risk as she gets closer to retirement.

Next, Eloise shopped around and interviewed a few financial advisors to help her understand her ideal investment mix and to walk her through her options. The one she chose determined that she should be ideally diversified for her time horizon, risk tolerance, and investment knowledge at 10 percent cash, 50 percent bonds, and 40 percent equities. However, she felt that 40 percent in equities was too risky, so she instead agreed to a 20 percent equity exposure and is slowly moving her cash over the next twenty-four months into a basket of ETFs invested in Canadian and global equities. At the end of that two-year period, she and her advisor will reassess her comfort in those stock markets.

It's been twelve months since and she's feeling fairly good about her investments. She checks her portfolio every other week just to peek in and see how they're doing. The first few months were rocky in the market and her monthly equity contributions kept showing a negative balance. She'd get a huge pit in her stomach and reach out to her advisor for reassurance. But within six months, she started to see positive returns and is now taking comfort in the fact that while the majority of her money is in fixed income and isn't earning much, it's doing better than earning nearly nothing in a savings account.

She's not sure if or when she'll be comfortable fully increasing her equity exposure to her advisor's suggested mix, but at least she has a reasonable and thoughtful plan of attack. She's also added $1,000 a month to her current savings and is noticing how buying lower in some months is like purchasing something on sale. She loves a good deal and this notion is starting to take root!

7

Turn Financial Frowns Upside Down

Katie was second in command as the administrator for one of the largest hospital groups in the country. While she excelled at her job and had made great accomplishments, she was not very confident when it came to finances. Although her position paid well, most of Katie's money decisions were driven by her fear of debt. She grew up listening to tense conversations about money between family members or with friends who struggled with long-term debt. Since then, she'd decided to be very careful with her own finances. It was the only way she knew how to ensure a financially secure future. Still, there were times when she couldn't sleep at night because she was so worried about her financial future.

Her fears had only grown during her last serious relationship more than a decade ago, which ended when she found out that her boyfriend was cheating on her financially: he had bought a cabin without her knowing about it and even a luxury motorcycle that he kept in his friend's garage. Feeling betrayed, Katie broke it off and had since struggled to trust others when it came to finances. She didn't even know how to broach the topic with her friends, never mind a potential mate. Meanwhile, her friends always seemed perfectly at ease with money talk.

Now, at forty-nine years old, Katie was super proud that she had no credit card debt, unlike others she knew. She was also on track to be mortgage free by fifty-five. But when she met with a financial advisor, he scolded her for not having savings and for paying down low-interest mortgage debt instead of investing. Wait, hadn't she been doing things the right way? She was so confused.

WHERE SHE WENT WRONG

Paying off your mortgage quickly is a noble goal. That said, it's important that you crunch the numbers and weigh all possible options. With historically low interest rates, it may be more prudent to pay down your mortgage *and* invest at the same time. After all, if you have a change in circumstances in the future, you can't eat your countertop.

Misstep #1: Letting Fear Take Control

Katie let her fear of debt and financial mismanagement rule all of her decisions, but she's not alone. Many women, particularly in midlife, cite money as a key issue keeping them up at night. An Allianz study of women with household incomes of $30,000 or higher found that 49 percent of respondents "often" or "sometimes" feared losing all their money and becoming homeless.[1] A third of these respondents had incomes of $200,000 or more. This is a real concern for women regardless of their incomes.

Misstep #2: Not Getting Professional Help

Many of Katie's fears could have been soothed if she had reached out to a professional advisor earlier. She occasionally spoke with a banker but never really sought out financial counsel. Years ago, she had met with a financial advisor referred to her by her dad, but he talked down to her and made her feel inferior. While he offered some good advice about investing, that experience made her never want to go back to him or consult someone else.

Katie's not alone in her disillusionment with and mistrust of the financial industry. Seventy-three percent of women report being "unhappy" with the financial services industry, and 80 percent of Canadian women switch advisors within a year of their husband's death.[2] It took years before Katie finally worked up the courage to see another advisor, and by then it was a bit late.

Misstep #3: Paying Off Her Mortgage Without Considering All the Options

Katie had an "away from" attitude, rather than a "towards" mindset, when it came to life and finances. Simply put, her decisions were motivated by things she wanted to avoid (get away from)—in particular, debt and financial uncertainty. She was so incredibly focused on paying down her debt and fast-tracking her mortgage freedom that she never considered putting her money towards investments that would bring her gains in the future. Her mortgage interest rate averaged less than 4 percent for the last fifteen years. This would have given her a great opportunity to divide up her money and invest some while still paying off her debts, but she didn't dare take that chance.

Misstep #4: Missing Out on Compounded Savings and Refunds

A moderate-risk investment portfolio over a ten-year period has historically earned 6 to 7 percent over the long run. As a benchmark for comparison, the Morningstar Canada Neutral Global Target Allocation Index has returned 7.1 percent over the past ten years, as of March 31, 2021. After fees, those mutual funds earned 5.9 percent. Given low interest rates and depending on fees, expectations for the next ten years are projected to be lower—around 4 or 5 percent—but it could still be a worthwhile and profitable investment, depending on her current mortgage interest rate.

Not only was Katie missing out on the investment's compounding over the past decade and a half, she also lost out on the tax refund that an RRSP would have provided.

Misstep #5: Not Knowing How to Discuss Money

Katie never learned how to talk about money with other people. In her previous relationship, she assumed her boyfriend shared her views on finance and was shocked when he made such large purchases behind her back. It hurt to be lied to, but this betrayal might have been avoided if they had spoken about their views on money earlier and agreed to be more transparent with each other.

Even though Katie was very close with her friends, she didn't feel comfortable discussing finances with them. They all seemed so confident with their own investments that she didn't dare admit her fears or areas of confusion.

THE SOLUTION?

It's crucial to examine all possible options when it comes to mortgages and investments, and to develop a plan that works best for you. Having a secure, well-conceived financial plan will allow you to keep a roof over your head while you also prepare for the future.

Step #1: Get a Clear Road Map for the Future

Much of Katie's anxiety would have been mitigated if she had a plan. A good financial plan is akin to a GPS: it lays out a clear path, based on your goals, for what you need to do and when, to make it to your destination. This can include a plan for retirement, saving for a home, getting married, or making sure your hard-earned dollars are taxed less and go to whom you desire at your death. Even if life takes you off course through job loss, divorce, or the death of a partner, a good financial planner can recalculate a new path for you.

Just about everyone over the age of eighteen should have a financial plan, but there are some challenges that might make people less inclined to actually get one and stick to it. I hear from readers regularly who when presented with a financial plan, they were given a twenty-page document that ultimately went unread, collecting dust in their drawer. Or they might have been given advice that felt nearly impossible to follow or such a bleak picture of their financial future that they never want to return.

It can be easy to feel defeated in these situations, but it's crucial that you keep looking for the right financial professional who will listen to your concerns and work with you to build a realistic and achievable plan. For example, a good planner knows the importance of reducing big steps into manageable tasks, like setting up an RRSP one month and maybe tackling your taxes a few months later, and so on.

What's in a financial plan?

A financial plan should include:

- a snapshot of your financial life
- your short- and long-term goals
- an analysis of your cash flow, debt, investments, insurance, tax reduction, and estate-planning strategies
- strategies for implementation

What should a financial plan cover?

- Budgeting and taxes
- Managing liquidity, or ready access to cash
- Financing plans for large purchases
- Managing your risk
- Investing your money
- Planning for retirement and the transfer of your wealth
- Communication and record keeping

Who offers a financial plan?

- Your bank, if you have investable assets
- Financial/investment advisors, as a value-add if you have investable assets
- A Qualified Associate Financial Planner (QAFP)
    - *These planners focus on less complex needs, such as investing in an RRSP or paying down your mortgage.*

- A Certified Financial Planner (CFP)
  - *These planners provide more comprehensive strategies, such as tax, estate, and retirement planning.*
- A fee-only financial planner
  - *QAFPs and CFPs can provide planning-only services, meaning that they don't sell any products (i.e., stocks, bonds, mutual funds, insurance, ETFs, etc.).*
- A portfolio manager (PM)
  - *PMs generally work with clients who have $500,000-plus in investable assets. They may or may not provide financial planning. If they're a larger PM, they may have a planner on staff included in your fees.*

What does a financial plan cost?

If you have at least $250,000 to invest, a planner at your bank or a QAFP or CFP who sells products will offer a basic or comprehensive financial plan as a value-added service.

If you have less than $250,000 to invest or want an objective third-party plan by someone who doesn't have a vested interest in the products you choose, you'll want to look for a fee-only QAFP or CFP. They may charge by the plan or by the hour. A comprehensive plan with a CFP usually costs about $2,000 to $5,000, depending on complexity. But you can find planners who charge by the hour, usually $150 to $250 per hour.

Are there other financial professionals to consider?

- Insurance professionals
  - *If you're looking for life, disability, or critical illness insurance, a QAFP/CFP may also be licensed to sell insurance.*

- Lawyers
    - *If you're drafting or updating your will, power of attorney, or personal directives (health care directives), you'll want to find a lawyer who specializes in estate planning.*
- Chartered Professional Accountants (CPAs)
    - *If you have complex needs, such as getting your money out of a corporation tax-efficiently at retirement or dealing with complicated investment holdings (i.e., rental properties, foreign properties, and more), you may occasionally want the opinion of a CPA.*

What questions should you ask?

Right now, most provinces allow anyone to call themselves a financial planner, without any education, experience, or professional designations, other than in Quebec. You must be very diligent and do your homework before investing with anyone. Financial planning is a complex and detailed process that requires a strong understanding of various topics, so be sure that your planner is properly trained and certified. Fraudsters abound, and once you give your money to a scammer, it's almost guaranteed you won't recover it. A little pre-work can protect you and your hard-earned money.

You should ask the planner:

- Their qualifications to offer financial advice. This can include the training they had to complete, if they hold any professional credentials, and how they stay up-to-date with changes in the financial planning field. You should also ask if they are regulated by any organization. Planners who sell financial products or give investment advice must be registered with provincial regulatory authorities. The CFP credential is internationally recognized as the sign of a professional financial planner.

- Their experience. This can include how many years they've practiced, the types of firms they have previously worked at, and whether they have any experience with clients in similar circumstances to your own. It's recommended that you choose a financial planner with at least three years of financial advising experience, which is also the minimum requirement needed for a CFP certification.
- The services they offer. We've already explored the various services above, but be sure you find an advisor who actually deals with the service you need.
- Whether they will be the only person working with you. It's common for planners to work with other professionals in their organization, so you may want to meet the entire team. If you already have a lawyer or accountant, the planner can also work with them.
- How much they charge and how you will pay them. This might be an hourly rate, a flat fee, a percentage from the commission of the products they sell you, or a percentage of the assets they are managing on your behalf.
- Whether anyone else will benefit from their recommendations. Conflicts of interest may lead to recommendations that are not in your best interest.[3]

A common complaint is that financial plans are used as a sales tool for insurance policies, RRSP loans, or other financial products. Note that fee-only financial planners do not sell financial products, but their planning comes at a cost. A free financial plan from a bank will likely sell financial products, with the planner taking a commission or some other incentive. Still, some advice is better than nothing. You are under no obligation to follow a free financial plan from a bank or financial advisor, by the way, so there's little harm in listening.

Be sure to ask any planner for a written agreement that lists all the services that will be provided. Keep this document in your files.

What if you only want to invest?

If you're only buying an investment and not necessarily in need of a financial plan, consider these questions before you proceed:

- How does this investment operate? How well do you understand the ins and outs? Be mindful that if you can't explain it to a friend, you don't understand it well enough and need to get more informed.
- Is this a short-, medium-, or long-term investment?
- What investments do you have already? How do any new investments fit with your prior investments? Is your entire investment portfolio well balanced?
- What are the risks of this investment? How comfortable are you with the risk level you're assuming? When you imagine a worst-case scenario, can you live with the loss?
- What are your goals? Are you looking for a slow and steady, low-risk investment, or is growth your main goal?
- How much do you expect to earn on this investment? Is this realistic?
- What are the costs (both transparent and hidden) to buy, hold, and sell the investment? Don't forget to calculate the taxes you'll pay on the money you earn.[4]

Last, check with reputable sources before you invest or settle on a planner or an advisor. Each province has a securities commission (e.g., the Alberta Securities Commission, the Ontario Securities Commission), and you'll want to ensure that you're working with someone who is registered and in good standing.

Here are some places you should check with:

- For investments: provincial securities commissions, Investment Industry Regulatory Organization of Canada, the Mutual Fund Dealers Association
- For insurance or insurance-type investments: provincial insurance councils
- For financial planners: FP Canada

Step #2: Understand Mortgages

Katie was fixated on paying off her mortgage as soon as possible, without being fully aware of all her payment options. Mortgages can seem intimidating, especially since it's probably one of the biggest purchases most people will ever make, but let's break it down.

The Basics

A mortgage is a long-term loan, generally from a bank, secured against your house, condo, etc. Without a product like a mortgage, most people would never be able to buy their own home or would spend decades saving up. It's made up of multiple components:

- **Amount borrowed:** The total amount you're seeking from the bank.
- **Down payment:** The amount of money you've saved. You generally need 5 percent at minimum as a down payment to buy a home you will live in, or 20 percent for a rental property or vacation property. For a conventional mortgage, you'll need 20 percent down. With a greater down payment, you'll have lower monthly payments and less time needed to pay it off.
- **Amortization:** The total amount of time it will take you to pay off your mortgage. Twenty-five years is often used, but you can pay your mortgage off sooner. The shorter your amortization, the higher your monthly payment. You can extend your amortization over thirty years if you have at least 20 percent equity in the property or a 20 percent down payment.
- **Term:** The amount of time your interest rate will be fixed rather than variable; you negotiate the term with your bank.

    - *Fixed- or closed-rate terms range from six months to ten years, and the interest rate is generally higher the longer your term. You're locked into your term, which means you're unable to break the contract without a penalty. That includes if you'd like to switch lenders or change your interest rate. Fixed rates are higher because you're basically buying insurance against the risk of interest rates' rising.*

- *Variable or open rates generally provide a lower interest rate than a fixed term. You are still locked into a term of several years, but your interest rate floats with the prime lending rate. If you're in an open-rate mortgage, you also pay a premium, as you are free to break the contract without penalty. Variable rates will generally net you the lowest interest costs over the life of your mortgage, unless interest rates jump. This can make variable rates a riskier option, as the price can change unexpectedly.*

As I write this, here's an example of some current mortgage interest rates:

- One-year closed: 2.79 percent
- Five-year closed: 4.59 percent (special offer advertised of 2.44 percent)
- Ten-year closed: 5.6 percent
- Five-year closed variable: 1.55 percent[5]

Open mortgages are good for someone who is expecting to pay their mortgage off right away, unsure about locking in, or planning to sell soon. However, if you're nervous about interest rates fluctuating and would prefer to know exactly what your mortgage rate is each month for budgeting purposes, a fixed-rate mortgage may be a better option.

I'd like to underscore that your mortgage rate is negotiable. You should absolutely shop around online and then have a conversation with your banker or a new bank to see how much you can negotiate the rate down. Even a quarter or half of a percent reduction can save you tens of thousands of dollars over the life of your mortgage. Many banks will also advertise special interest rates throughout the year, so hop online often if you're in the market for a new home or mortgage renewal.

If you're not comfortable with haggling, you may wish to reach out to a mortgage broker. These pros will help you shop the lending market and present you with the best possible rates.

You have many options as to how often you'll make your mortgage payments. You can pay them once a month, every two weeks, or even weekly. If you pay weekly, you'll make an extra payment or two per year, so it accelerates how fast you're paying your mortgage and thus lowers how much interest you pay. It will cost you the most interest to pay monthly, but if that's how you receive your paycheque, it may make sense to stick with monthly payments.

Let's look at how these numbers play out, based on the average price of a house in Canada, as of April 15, 2021:

- House price of $716,826
- 20 percent down payment = $143,365.20
- $573,460.80 mortgage
- Five-year fixed term at 4.59 percent (assuming there wasn't a special rate offer)

Frequency	Payment	Total Payments	Interest Paid	Principal Paid	Balance at the End of the Term
Monthly	$3,202.70	$192,162.00	$122,929.32	$69,232.68	$504,227.32
Biweekly	$1,472.39	$191,410.70	$122,344.67	$69,066.03	$504,393.97
Weekly	$735.88	$191,328.80	$122,261.19	$69,067.61	$504,392.39

You'll see that you save $584.65 in interest over a five-year fixed term by paying biweekly instead of monthly, and $668.13 if you decide to pay weekly instead of monthly. It doesn't sound like a lot, but it adds up over a twenty-five-year amortization. Plus, if your mortgage amount is higher and the interest rate increases after your term, paying more frequently saves you money over time.

Most mortgages allow you to prepay 10 or 20 percent per year without penalty and to double up on your payments, but you should check your mortgage agreement or ask your lender for details.

Step #3: Weigh the Pros and Cons of Investing Versus Fast-Tracking Mortgage Payments

As we've seen above, there is a great benefit to paying off your mortgage faster, as you will pay a lot less in interest over the term.

If you're comfortable investing in a moderate- or aggressive-risk portfolio, especially with the tax benefits of an RRSP or TFSA, it's not unreasonable to expect that those investments could earn more than the interest on your mortgage. This could add tens of thousands of dollars to your overall net worth over a decade or more. Of course, that's not guaranteed. If your investment fees are high, it may be tougher to earn a better return than your mortgage rate over the long run. And if you're a conservative investor, paying down debt may not be a bad "investment" alternative.

If you can earn a higher return on your investments than your mortgage rate, you may come out ahead over the long run, especially if your tax rate is high now and you expect it to be low at retirement.

Step #4: Figure Out Your Financial Fidelity

Financial infidelity is a common issue for couples. A 2018 study revealed that 53 percent of participants said they had kept money secrets, such as hiding receipts or lying about the price of an item, from their partner. However, only 27 percent admitted to having committed a financial infidelity.

Often when people partner up, the money game gets complicated, as everyone has different ideas of how to best use their funds—and you might not always agree. It's vital to discuss finance as early as possible in your relationship so everyone is clear on where they stand and these types of situations can be avoided. Consider how you want to share money. Some couples share everything fifty-fifty, including their bills, income, and spending, but have no discretionary spending of their own. On the opposite side are the couples that share absolutely nothing; they may split some bills but their incomes and assets are otherwise separate. Most couples fall somewhere in between, with a joint operating account for day-to-day purchases and bills, and separate bank accounts for other purchases.

Keep Communicating

Remember that incomes will never remain constant over the span of a long-term relationship and that you may need to regularly evaluate whether your current financial situation makes sense. Even with separate bank accounts, it will help to be transparent about big purchases that might ultimately affect you both.

Step #5: Find a Money Buddy

If you're struggling financially, finding a money buddy or support group to share your struggles with can ease your anxiety and provide much-needed encouragement as you get back on your feet. If you're like Katie and don't have anyone to discuss money matters with, or feel overwhelmed talking about it with people you know well, start a Facebook group, start an investment club (formal or informal), or reach out to those you admire on LinkedIn for support.

WHERE IS SHE NOW?

Katie never realized what a difference crunching numbers could have made to her bottom line. The good news is that she's leaning into financial literacy instead of avoiding it. All she needed was a financial advisor who respected her and motivated her to dig into the topic.

Before choosing a planner, she interviewed three pros and some of their clients. She settled on Jaimy because she made Katie feel super comfortable and, more important, showed her that there are a number of paths to her future success. As a fee-only planner, Jaimy mapped out several options for Katie: fast-tracking paying down the mortgage for the next six years, maximizing investing, and options in between.

Jaimy helped Katie open a low-fee robo account that took care of all her investing needs. It took less than fifteen minutes to set it up and start to automate her savings. Katie also agreed to keep fast-tracking the mortgage payments, but to ease up a bit and allocate those extra dollars to her RRSP.

Jaimy hosted a virtual financial support group for women each month, and Katie decided to give it a try. The women shared their fears and worries about money. Katie felt comforted by their stories and the realization that she wasn't alone, and Jaimy provided many helpful tips at the group sessions.

After a year of attending these group meetings and several tweaks to her financial plan, Katie now feels confident about her finances. She loves checking her investment account to see how quickly it's adding up.

Her virtual group gals have a savings goal challenge of each saving $10,000 this year. Katie's not sure she'll make it to the goal, but it's super fun trying. For the first time in her life, she no longer fears money. These days, she sleeps really well and wakes up refreshed, knowing her future looks brighter than ever.

The Busy Breadwinner

At forty-eight years old, Amma had been rocking her career for more than a decade as the head of communications and marketing for a successful tech company. Recently, she'd been promoted to vice-president. She was confident, self-assured, and the financial head of her household.

She loved the idea of being a money boss, but she was not entirely certain she was one. Sure, she earned the money, but was she really the boss of it? She'd financially bailed out her husband, Bryan, when they got married. He arrived with a lot of money baggage after his messy divorce. After all, shouldn't they both enter a relationship with a clean slate? Now, after years of being together, Bryan wasn't well. He had a health condition that meant he hadn't been able to work for more than five years. Amma loved and adored him, but looking after him and their teenage twins was a lot. Plus, she was concerned about the future.

Their twin boys brought loads of joy to their family, but Amma worried that Bryan spoiled them too much and they weren't learning the financial basics her grandma had taught her growing up. Amma also had some amazing work perks, such as a pension and matching programs, but she wasn't aware that she was leaving free money on the table.

WHERE SHE WENT WRONG

Amma's a super-busy mom with many financial misconceptions that are holding her back from realizing her full wealth potential now and at retirement. She's at the perfect age and income level to make significant gains if she pays attention to her investments and recognizes her own blind spots.

Misstep #1: Bailing Out Her Husband After His Divorce

After her husband split with his first wife, any assets he had went to their settlement and legal costs. When the dust settled, he still owed $42,000 and he had zero assets at fifty-two years old. Amma wanted a clean slate for their relationship, so she drained a good chunk of her savings to pay off his debt. Little did she know that years later, she would need that money when he wasn't able to work anymore due to health issues. Hindsight, as they say, is twenty-twenty. You know what else is? A healthy emergency savings account.

Misstep #2: Failing to Tax-Plan for the Future

Amma's made a lot of smart moves in her life: great job, superior pension, investing in RRSPs, and more. But because she's the breadwinner of her family, all of the family assets are essentially in her name, making her tax situation a challenge. If she doesn't start planning soon, she'll be paying a maximum amount of tax in her retirement years and may miss out on some government benefits available to her when she retires.

Misstep #3: Letting Teens Have a Free Financial Ride

It frustrates Amma to no end that her two teenagers are downright financially spoiled. It seems she's always the one saying no to their every whim while her husband, Bryan, supports their "live for now" lifestyle. Here's the thing: he has no idea about their family finances. The little income he receives is lavished on the boys. If she doesn't teach them financial literacy while they're still home, how will they ever handle credit cards and learn to save and spend prudently in the future? She worries her kids are learning the wrong lessons and yet she's afraid to be the boss of them. She hasn't had the tough-love conversation with her husband or children because she wants to keep the peace—sometimes, though, it comes at too high a cost.

Misstep #4: Spending Now on a Future That May Not Exist

Amma and her mom bought a condo in Greece a few years ago. The plan was for her mom to live there and rent it out until Amma retired, at which time she and Bryan would join her there. But Amma's mother suffered some health problems and had to come back home. Still, they have a joint mortgage on the property, and it nags at Amma that she's wasting money every month on the mortgage and interest on a vacant, unrented property.

Misstep #5: Being Haphazard with Charitable Donations

Giving back to charity is a significant priority for Amma. Her grandma often told her about the financial backers who helped her family come to and settle in Canada as immigrants. She's never forgotten those early lessons of community. But she does feel that the twins aren't learning those lessons. She wants to involve them more in her philanthropic pursuits, but they don't seem interested. She donates a few hundred dollars a year to dozens of small volunteer efforts. Maybe it's more than she can afford, but she can't say no to a good cause. The problem is, she also can't seem to say no when her boys promise to help with charitable efforts and then back out at the last minute every time.

Misstep #6: Not Talking Money with Her Husband

Amma loves her husband dearly, but he's clueless about their finances. It's exhausting for her to manage everything, and while he can't work because of his physical limitations, he can definitely learn more about their money situation. At the very least, he should know what financial institutions she deals with, what professionals she uses, and where their important documents are stored. She also needs to help him get his own credit card. He's currently using a supplementary card on her account and if she passed away, he'd have no credit established in his name.

Every time Amma brings up money, her husband makes an excuse to leave the room or changes the subject. She knows the topic is stressful for him—but hey, it's stressful for her, too! And this is one burden that should be shared between them instead of landing fully on her shoulders. Still, she lets him get away with this behaviour each and every time because she doesn't want to seem domineering. There's just one problem: avoidance is helping no one.

Misstep #7: Not Hiring Out or Asking for Help to Free Up Time

Bryan feels bad on a daily basis that he's not bringing in any income. He tries his best to help around the house, but his health suffers as a result. Whenever housework, cooking, grocery shopping, lawn care, or snow removal needs to be done, Bryan is adamant that he'll do it but often he simply can't. This means Amma returns home after a day's work to . . . more work. Lately, she's asking herself if she can manage it all. She isn't getting any younger and that feeling grows stronger every day. Amma knows the boys should help out but feels guilty about adding to their load when school should be their priority. So, she sucks it up while everyone sucks the life out of her. Doesn't she deserve some free time, too?

Misstep #8: Not Digging into Her Company Matching Programs

Usually meticulous with her money, Amma never seems to get to that to-do list item of digging into her company benefits and matching program. She has a group RRSP started and remembers seeing an email about a group TFSA but doesn't think much about it. Then, life gets busy, and she keeps procrastinating. What Amma doesn't realize is she's leaving free money on the table that could add to her bottom line and wealth in the future.

Amma's lucky that her company automatically enrolled her in its pension plan, which is estimated to provide her with a significant income when she retires. But she doesn't know there's a tax hit lurking in her future.

Misstep #9: Ignoring Estate Planning

Anxiety bubbles up every so often when Amma considers her own mortality. Sometimes she panics about what would happen if she died today. She's never drafted her will or power of attorney and doesn't want Bryan to be stranded. He has almost no income, and she desperately wants the kids to be protected against every eventuality, too. She doesn't know what she can leave to them and what she can't. She also worries that if she sets them up for financial success after her passing, they may have it too easy. What if they marry and then divorce someone who gets the spoils of *her* lifetime of toil? A real money boss would know how to deal with this. Does Amma? Not really.

THE SOLUTION?

Getting your financial life in order when there are added complexities, such as tax and estate planning and family health issues, can seem overwhelming. But it doesn't have to be. You first need to know what you don't know and then start reorganizing your finances by breaking down the problem areas into manageable action steps.

Step #1: Understanding What You're Financially Agreeing to When You Say "I Do"

If you entered into a relationship like Amma and Bryan's where one partner has significant debt, you need to know your rights, your responsibilities, and how to proceed in collaboration.

If a partner has debt that you didn't participate in or co-sign for, you are not accountable for it while together or even if you separate. That's not to say that if your partner defaults, collection agencies won't try to come after you. But you're not on the hook for debt you didn't sign for and that was incurred prior to the beginning of your relationship. You're also not responsible for any debt your spouse or partner applied for that you didn't participate in during your relationship. If you didn't sign or co-sign for the debt, it's their burden—not yours.

In the case of Amma, she really desired buying a home with

Bryan and creating a fresh start in their relationship. She didn't want him to file for bankruptcy because that would have hurt their ability to obtain a mortgage together.

If you're entering into debt with another person, it's vital to know that the responsibility is not fifty-fifty. It's actually 100 percent on both sides. This is debt that you both are applying for and agreeing to. If your partner defaults, you're 100 percent on the hook for the repayment, and vice versa.

Step #2: Teach Your Kids About Money

Allow me to present my simple system to teach your kids financial literacy.

Finance for Kids

Age 5 and under: Get a piggy bank. The idea at this age is simply to introduce your children to cash and currency. Every dollar your child receives from gifts can go in their piggy bank, and allow them to empty it as often as they'd like to buy things that are fun. If giving back is important to you and your family, perhaps suggest a split of fifty-fifty to your kids: half for their enjoyment and half for giving back or for those less fortunate in their community.

Ages 6–10: Keep the first piggy bank and get a second one. As your child might now be receiving an allowance or more money from family birthday gifts, it's time to help them divvy up their income and set short-term goals. Do they have a swim or ski pass they want to save up for in the coming months? How much should they put in their fun spending bank and how much into their short-term savings? The idea here is to teach your child that there are expenses you can anticipate with planning and others that need to be saved for.

Ages 11–16: It's time for a real bank account. As your child is receiving and possibly earning more money, they need to learn how to bank. Introduce a long-term savings element. For example, they still need to save up for the swim or ski pass (short-term savings), but they also have a school trip to Europe coming up in a year or two. You'll want to help them visualize their goal (create a goal thermometer) and ways to creatively earn more income to raise funds. How will they split their income into fun spending, short-term savings, and long-term savings (skills they'll need as an adult)? And let's not forget giving to others, too. Continue the idea of a donation to a charity of their choice. If they keep up good grades for a semester, consider rewarding them with a matching contribution and also a little something for their bank account.

Age 16+: Keep all the previous accounts and add a mock credit card. Let's say a new pair of Rollerblades is on sale and you are willing to buy them for your child—on a credit loan from the Bank of Mom and Dad. Set terms and a very attractive low interest rate, with penalties for default. The idea here isn't to profit from your child, but to get them understanding the real-life terms of how credit works. Better now with a forgiving lender than later! You might even consider that once the debt is paid off and your child has met all their financial obligations, the interest you earned can be returned to them. Just make sure they realize no creditor will ever be so lenient!

Amma wants the boys to know that there are income opportunities for people tuned into the market. She needs the twins to understand that chores come with being part of the family and aren't always paid, but that they can also earn more if they do more than the minimum. She sat down with them on the weekend to brainstorm a list of all possible assignments above and beyond what was expected. Motivated by extra earnings, they came up with quite a list:

- Cleaning the garage
- Cleaning the pantry and donating unused canned goods to their local food bank
- Mowing the lawn and shoveling the snow
- Helping their elderly neighbours with yard work for payment
- Polishing Mom's shoes
- Organizing the junk drawers
- Selling old stuff online

The boys took on more responsibility and, after a while, they even lost some of the snark that had previously come with every request for free money from her wallet. It took some time and patience, but she now feels they're starting to learn that money is effort-earned and that their participation in the functioning of the household influences what she's willing to finance for them.

Step #3: Plan for Taxes Now and in the Future

Tax-planning now means potentially paying less tax in the future. But you often can't wait until a year or two before retirement when strategies like income splitting with your spouse must be done years before. If you're the higher-income earner now or will have more or the bulk of the income in your name as opposed to your spouse's at retirement, it makes sense to explore income-splitting strategies.

There are options such as spousal RRSPs, having the high-income spouse pay the family expenses and the low-income spouse save in their name, prescribed-rate loans, or family trusts to split income with not only your spouse but also potentially your kids.

In Amma's case, she should have been considering income-splitting options like setting up a spousal RRSP for Bryan or lending money to him to invest. She has no plans of divorcing him, so she needs to worry less about putting assets in her name. She could invite him to learn about investing basics and include him in her meetings with her financial planner. As he learns more, he will likely want to participate more fully in their finances, alleviating her fears that he'll blow all their assets if she passes away.

A prescribed-rate loan is when a high-income spouse loans money to a low-income spouse to invest. If a high-income spouse just gives money to a low-income spouse to invest, there's a concept called attribution where the resulting income is attributed back to the high-income spouse. A loan at the prescribed interest rate—currently 1 percent—allows the income earned in excess of that rate to be basically moved from one spouse to the other.

A spousal RRSP allows you to put money in your spouse's name. You receive the tax deduction, but at retirement, the income upon withdrawal is taxable to your spouse. This is a good idea if you think your spouse will be in a lower tax bracket than you at retirement. The higher-income spouse contributes to a spousal RRSP and claims the tax deduction on their own tax return. The lower-income spouse can withdraw that money in the future in retirement.

Tax-planning is beyond the scope of this book, but consider it an important element in your retirement and estate plan. Sit down with a qualified Chartered Professional Accountant and a fee-only Certified Financial Planner to work out a plan just for you.

- You receive the tax deduction
- Investments owned by your spouse
- Withdrawals will be taxed in the hands of your spouse
- Deposits are based on your contribution room
- Ideal for tax splitting

Step #4: Understand Foreign Property Law If You Own a Property in Another Country

A common misconception is that foreign income is not taxable. In fact, Canadians are often taxed on their worldwide income, and that includes foreign property. There are reporting requirements annually on your tax return for foreign assets in excess of $100,000 with steep penalties for failure to report. Tax paid in another country can generally be claimed on your Canadian tax return as a foreign tax credit to avoid double taxation. An exception may apply if it's a pension or similar tax-sheltered account. Rental properties are subject to capital gains tax upon sale.

Amma finally decided to sell her property in Greece. After the Realtor and other costs, her capital gain was $200,000 (the difference between what she paid for the condo and what she sold it for, less her mortgage). She had to report the gain on her taxes the next year but still netted $150,000. Now she's meeting with her financial advisor to see how she can maximize those dollars in Canadian investments.

Step #5: Create a Charitable Giving Plan

Giving to charities is a noble endeavour. When planning to give, you can receive that tax break while you're alive (receiving the tax reduction now) or at death (reducing the overall tax owing on your estate). The tax credit you'll receive depends on your tax bracket (a tax credit reduces your overall tax owing but can't generate a tax refund like a deduction can).

Taxable Income Up to $200,000

As an example, a donor in Alberta with a taxable income of $40,000 makes a donation of $700 in 2020. Their tax credit is calculated as the total of:

Federal charitable donation tax credit

- $30 (15 percent on the first $200)
- $145 (29 percent on the remaining $500)

$175 ($30 + $145) is their total federal tax credit.

Provincial charitable donation tax credit

- $20 (10 percent on the first $200)
- $105 (21 percent on the remaining $500)

$125 ($20 + $105) is their total provincial tax credit.

Therefore, $300 ($175 + $125) is their total charitable donation tax credit for 2016.

What and how can you donate

- Give cash.
- Give stocks and other assets "in kind," meaning you transfer them to the charity "as is" instead of selling them and giving cash.
- Name a charity as beneficiary for your life insurance. If you name a charity as the beneficiary of your insurance policy, the annual premiums may be considered a charitable donation. Alternatively, if you have your insurance paid into your estate and then use some or all of it to make a donation, that donation can save you tax on your final tax return.

If you and your family wish to leave a larger legacy, you may wish to start a foundation or utilize a community foundation in your city to set up a fund. Both allow you to make decisions on whom your money will go to while you're alive and after you pass away.

Step #6: Know When to Hire Out

Many studies suggest that women spend more than 50 percent more time doing unpaid work than men, while men spend 37 percent more time doing income-generating activities.[1]

Amma knows she's doing far too much around the house and it's affecting her ability at times to focus on her work and well-being. As she's recently been promoted at work to a VP position, she has many more responsibilities on her plate. When she has to cook and clean after a long day, it leaves very little time and energy for her hobbies or to spend time with the boys on their homework.

She should consider the cost of her time versus the energy and expense for the following and where she can hire these duties out:

- Laundry/dry cleaning (many will deliver for free)
- Biweekly or monthly house cleaning, especially spring and fall cleaning
- Meal prep delivery kits
- Grocery delivery
- A tax preparer to do her, Bryan's, and her mom's taxes each year
- Ubers for the boys' marital arts classes
- Lawn and snow maintenance

Take an honest look at the time you spend in a given month around your house and with your family. Are there family members who can and should be contributing more? Can you realign the household work, splitting it up between you? If not, can you afford to get outside help?

Spend some time researching what it would cost to hire some services. Meal kits, dry cleaning and grocery delivery, lawn and snow care, and housekeeping are all great areas to research. If you're trading time for money, as most of us do, be diligent about the value of your time.

Step #7: Take Advantage of Employer Incentives

If you work for a company that offers benefits, please dig into them. Some benefits your work may provide include:

- Accidental death and dismemberment coverage
  - *Coverage usually varies from $50,000 to $100,000.*
- Employee and family assistance program

  - *This can include work-life and wellness support such as nutritional counselling, smoking cessation and weight loss consultations, mental health support, and more.*
- Flex plan benefits
  - *Benefits can cover ambulance, hospital, extended health, dental, and more.*
- Wellness and sustainability account
  - *These accounts encourage healthy living for employees and can offset the costs of physical activity, wellness programs, recycling, and more.*
- Home insurance
  - *Discounts may be available as an employee.*
- Life insurance
  - *Often your employer will pay for your basic coverage and you can elect to pay for optional coverage. Sometimes you can obtain spousal coverage as well. If you have a pre-existing medical condition that could make it hard to get life insurance, group life insurance often has no medical requirement up to certain dollar limits.*
- Long-term disability insurance
  - *Your employer may pay for your long-term disability insurance. The purpose is to provide you with monthly income if you become totally disabled and remain disabled for an extended period of time.*
  - *If your employer pays, that's great, but note that if you ever have to collect, the income is taxable to you. If you pay the premiums yourself, any disability income you receive is tax-free. Keep that in mind when you're evaluating whether you have enough coverage.*
- Retirement benefits
  - *Pensions*

    - Defined contribution (DC) pensions are where you choose your investment options, which by default are usually mutual funds (unknown end benefit at retirement)
    - Defined benefit (DB) pensions are controlled by your employer and where you receive a monthly pension in retirement based on a formula (known end benefit at retirement)
  - *Group registered retirement savings plan*
  - *Group tax-free savings*
- Voluntary benefits
  - *This could include group discounts for travel, health plans, your home and cell phone, and more. Some plans also offer critical illness (CI) protection that pays out a lump-sum benefit if you develop a covered critical illness.*

As we examined in chapter 5, if you're not traditionally employed because you're an entrepreneur or in the gig economy, you may wish to get your own insurance or set up automatic savings to mimic a pension plan. Disability and life insurance should be your first priority, with health and dental as a secondary matter. Think about the benefits as well from joining your local chamber of commerce or professional associations, as they often offer discounted services to replace what you might be offered as an employee.

Step #8: Have a Family Money Talk and Create an Estate Binder

The thought of working hard for your money only to have it squandered when you pass away is frustrating at best, futile at worst. And as the saying goes, where there's a will, there's a relative.

Making your final wishes known to family can be a tense conversation that may need to be had in several sit-downs and perhaps with the help of a professional financial planner or counsellor.

Not educating your family as to the assets you're leaving them (including hard assets such as investments and real estate, but also life insurance policies and other benefits) can leave them vulnerable to fraudsters who unscrupulously scour obituaries to then prey on grieving family members.

Take time to at the very least create a binder of your accounts and professionals. You don't have to list the passwords and shouldn't. But it's ideal that you have an accordion file or binder that spells out what you have and don't have. It should include:

- a list of all of your bank and investment accounts
- all of your registered assets and account numbers (RRSPs, TFSAs, etc.)
- digital accounts such as robo-investments or cryptocurrency holdings
- your pension information and contact person
- your professionals (banker, lawyer, financial planner, advisor)
- location of your will, power of attorney, and living will
- location of your safety deposit box key
- a declaration of what passwords are written out and held for safekeeping in your safety deposit box

Be sure to also make a list of what you don't have, such as a will, power of attorney, etc. That way, your loved ones won't be looking for something that doesn't exist.

Step #9: Start Your Estate Planning Now

Almost everyone over the age of eighteen should have a will. This is a document that outlines your wishes at death and who should receive your assets, cherished items, and more. If you have children or a pet, you'll want to appoint a guardian and financial provisions for their care. An executor is someone (it can be a trust company or a lawyer, too) who will ensure your wishes are fulfilled at your death as instructed by your will. It's not an enviable position to be named to. The executor has a fiduciary obligation to comply with the instructions for the disbursement of assets, pay debts, file tax returns, and more. If they're negligent, they can be held financially accountable. Your executor should know that they're named in your will and where to find a copy. There should be a copy of your will kept in your safety deposit box or locked up at home, with your lawyer keeping the original. If your financial affairs are simple and you don't have dependents, a will kit or online will service may suffice. In some provinces, you can hand-write and sign your will (called a holographic will).

A power of attorney (POA) is a written document that grants someone authorization to act on your behalf in some matter (legal, financial, business, real estate, etc.) while you're alive. For strictly financial decisions, most banks have their own power of attorney form that is restricted to the dealings of accounts and assets with them only. A POA ceases to exist when you die and then the will kicks in. The will bears no relevance while you're alive. Even if you're young and in excellent health, you may wish to have a power of attorney drafted in the event of an accident where you can't make financial decisions temporarily. The person you name in your power of attorney should know that they've been named and have a copy of the document. If it's locked away in your safety deposit box, they won't be able to get into it to prove they're named as your financial decision maker.

Note that different provinces have different estate-planning documents. In Ontario, powers of attorney for property and personal care are used to appoint people to make decisions about your finances and your health if you cannot. In other provinces, there are similar documents called personal directives, mandates, or representation agreements. They all accomplish similar goals: appointing someone to make decisions for you if you are alive but unable to make decisions because of injury, illness, or other incapacity.

A living will or personal directive states what health care and end-of-life considerations you'd like carried out. Your living will should also be known to your advocates and a copy provided to them. You may wish to put a copy in your car and/or in an easily accessible part of your home in the event of a health crisis or emergency.

Amma finally researched and met with a fee-only Certified Financial Planner. The planner helped her draft her will and a living will for her mom. Then the planner introduced her to an estate-planning lawyer who finalized the documents and her wishes. It was a huge relief to get this off her to-do list!

Organize Your Beneficiaries

A beneficiary is someone you name to receive your assets when you pass away. If you don't name one, in most provinces, your assets will go to your spouse (as with an RRSP) or be divided between your spouse and children, if you have them. However, a lack of clear guidelines can create a real strain for your family during a difficult time and leave questions about your wishes in the event of your death.

If you have conflicting beneficiary designations on assets such as your RRSP or pension and within your will, that can also cause great confusion and may result in your assets not going to whom you wished. Add it to your to-do list to check the beneficiaries on your RRSP accounts, TFSAs, life insurance, pension, will, and more. Make sure they're up-to-date and that the will reflects the elections you've made.

Some people name their young children as beneficiaries. If you're naming a minor to receive your assets, they will be held in trust by the province until they attain the age of majority. A better strategy is to consider making the funds payable to your estate and then establishing a trust in your will for your kids. You'll also need to name a trustee in this scenario. A lawyer can help you make these declarations and a financial professional can walk you through the pros and cons of each alternative.

WHERE IS SHE NOW?

It's been a few years and Amma can confidently say that finances are on the menu during many of her family's dinners. She's able to enjoy those mealtime experiences now that the twins help out more around the house. She brings in a housekeeper once a week for deep-cleaning, which has given her more time to herself, too. She's even been back at her book club!

Amma now has more time to double down on her job, which has paid off! She was recently promoted to senior vice-president at the tech company where she works. The promotion brought a juicy salary increase and a higher bonus. Now that the company is soaring, she even has stock options, which she's researched so she understands them fully.

Her financial planner has become a trusted advisor, and Amma talks to her a few times a month. Bryan has taken a real interest in the spousal RRSPs. Now that he has some skin in the game, he's paying more attention to their accounts and monitoring their finances. He and Amma actually have a little friendly rivalry about whose portfolio is doing better. It makes her so relieved that if something were to happen to her now, Bryan has a stronger financial foundation.

The boys really took to Amma's financial lessons and challenges. They still have goal thermometers in their rooms. As a total surprise to Amma, one of their short-term goals was raising money for a full spa day for her. After a quasi-edible Mother's Day breakfast in bed, they presented her with this amazing gift. She was delighted by the spa day, but the truth is that the better gift was seeing her sons' pride in giving back.

At long last, she really feels like the boss of things. Her career, her household, and the family finances are finally humming in unity. The future looks bright for her and for her family.

9

Digging Yourself Out of Debt

Krista always felt like money was burning a hole in her pocket. Her parents were great budgeters, but she wanted to throw caution to the wind with her finances. After all, you only get to live once, right?

When Krista received her first credit card at the age of twenty, the limit felt to her like a target to hit. She spent like mad. Then she had her first child, got married, and had another child a couple of years later. After a messy divorce, Krista was insolvent, unable to pay her bills. She found herself in her midthirties with more than $50,000 in debt. With no other options in sight, she filed for bankruptcy. She was a single mom, alone with no assets, and her only suitors were angry collections callers. She felt like a total failure.

She had a great job with the provincial government as an auditor and co-workers who looked up to her; they didn't know about her debts and what a "loser" she felt she was. At night, Krista lay awake in her bed as the same questions looped over and over in her mind: "How is it that I'm now forty-five and unlike everyone else around me, my financial life is still a mess? When am I ever going to grow up?"

WHERE SHE WENT WRONG

If you've ever felt like a failure with your finances or the only person to ever hit rock bottom, you're not alone. Here's a thought to ease your mind: We don't learn financial smarts in school. There's no class that teaches you fiscal prudence, financial concepts, or how to manage your money—even though this is a baseline component of adult life! And guess what? Lots of people have been where you're at right now, and it's not too late to learn. Sometimes catching a financial misstep early can save money, stress, and heartache. But know that no matter your money woes, there's always a solution!

Misstep #1: Spending to the Limit

If you've ever felt like Krista and that a credit card limit is actually a baseline for your spending, it's time for a rethink. Many people fall into the trap of spending money they haven't yet earned, but it's crucial to set a spending limit.

Your real financial baseline consists of your monthly obligations and should be set using the following criteria:

- Your fixed costs, such as rent or mortgage payments, condo fees, utilities, cell phone, groceries, gas, etc.
- Your fixed debt costs, such as a car and student loans, line of credit, other debt servicing
- A percentage, calculated only after you've calculated your baseline in the steps above, for savings (if possible)

Add these up and there's your monthly financial threshold. Whatever you have left after paying for these essentials (and maybe socking some away)—not the amount of your available credit on your credit cards or line of credit—is money you can use on wants such as dining out, leisure activities, and shopping. If you don't have any funds left after adding up the above, you'll need to take a hard look at finding ways to reduce those expenses. Regardless of what you spend it on, you must learn to set your own limits and trust no bank or credit card to do it for you.

Misstep #2: Making YOLO–"You Only Live Once"–an Excuse for Debt

Krista believed in YOLO before Drake was on *Degrassi*. Her parents were so balanced with their finances, they never splurged or enjoyed a night out. Did she resent their frugality? Yes. When she thinks about this, she realizes that her parents' thriftiness led to her rebelliously swinging the pendulum the other way the moment she hit adulthood. Unfortunately, her spending habits were over the top, and she amassed debt irresponsibly.

Krista's first credit card was addictive. It was like free money available to tick items off her bucket list. Because she had a steady job and great credit, her bank kept upping her limit and other credit card offers came in regularly. Her bank even offered her a juicy line of credit of $20,000. It was irresistible to her and her then-husband. They spent the money on their wants nearly as fast as the credit was approved.

Misstep #3: Taking on the Full Burden of Debt in Marriage

Krista's divorce cost her much more than a broken heart. She lost the financial support of her husband, and that left her in a pit of debt. It's a common belief that women make out like bandits in divorce, but that's simply untrue. According to Stephen Jenkins, a professor at the London School of Economics, "women who worked before, during, or after their marriages see a 20 percent decline in income when their marriages end."[1] His research found that men's incomes rise more than 30 percent after divorce. Additionally, the poverty rate for separated women is 27 percent, nearly triple the figure for separated men.

During their marriage, Krista's then-partner had helped pay for half their expenses. But he stopped working during their divorce and was relying on government benefits to get by. Since he had no income, she didn't bother to take him to court for spousal support. She was exhausted from the divorce process and felt that even if she received a judgment against him, he wouldn't pay. But without his income, she couldn't make ends meet and fell behind on all her debts. Because she was the one with the secure job and stellar credit rating when they were together, she acquired all their debt in her name. Now she was the one holding the bag.

Misstep #4: Not Understanding the Crippling Long-Term Impact of Credit Card Interest

Have you ever heard of the Rule of 72? It's a lovely math shortcut. Seventy-two divided by your rate of return equals the number of years for your money to double. If you earn 7.2 percent as a rate of return, your money will double every ten years. This also works to help you understand how high-interest-rate credit cards can double your debt rapidly. Of the $50,000 debt Krista has, $30,000 is in credit card debt. Assuming an average interest rate of 18.5 percent, if she only makes the minimum payments, it will take her twenty-seven years to pay the debt off and she'll have shelled out $31,292.92 in interest (on top of the $30,000 she owed). You can see how the credit card companies cash in on this doubling rule when you owe.

Before Krista's bankruptcy, she seemed to be indebted everywhere. All her credit cards, utility bills, and other obligations were overdue, but she also owed money to her dad and friends. She could barely stand to see them for visits. Her guilt overwhelmed her, and she never brought the subject of repayment up. Her parents stood by her, but she lost a few very dear friends.

Misstep #5: Borrowing More Just Because She Could

Krista had lots of financial red flags that should have alerted her to change her habits. Some were subtle, such as using one credit card to pay the minimum payment of the other. This caused her to lose sleep and take her money worries to work.

Krista's not alone in fretting at the office over her finances. A recent survey from the Canadian Payroll Association found that 43 percent of workers are so financially stressed that their work performance is suffering.[2] Out of the more than four thousand respondents, nearly a quarter said they lose forty minutes each day at work to being distracted by personal financial matters. That equates to an 8.1 percent loss of productivity based on an eight-hour workday, which the association said adds up to an economic blow of $15.8 billion in lost productivity.

Shockingly, even with the stacks of debt most Canadians are dealing with, a recent survey found 60 percent of respondents would go into further debt to buy things they can't afford simply because interest rates are so low.[3]

Misstep #6: The Cost of Not Planning for Kids

Krista never dreamed of raising two young kids on her own. Although she had a great job, the costs of daycare and maintaining a home on her solo salary left more unpaid bills than money at the end of the month. Her monthly shortfall was more than $1,200 and she racked up debt on her line of credit to pay for groceries, extracurricular activities for the kids, and to simply get by. She knew that lifeline wouldn't last, but she couldn't see another choice.

When she and her ex decided to officially divorce, a lawyer friend of hers agreed to help her out for free. It wasn't the lawyer's specialty, and she simply filed the documents to make the process official. She encouraged Krista to take her ex to court for formal child support, but Krista didn't have the emotional bandwidth or money to hire a qualified lawyer to see her through the process. This meant her ex wasn't legally being forced to support Krista and the kids. Feeling she had no other options, she declared bankruptcy. She thought this was the new start and clean slate she needed. What she didn't realize is that bankruptcy comes at a high cost.

Misstep #7: Digging Herself into Debt . . . Again

After declaring bankruptcy, it took years for Krista to qualify for a credit card and line of credit again. Fast-forwards to twelve years after her bankruptcy, and she found herself remarried . . . to a spender. Her new husband's income helped but they still fell short every month on expenses and resorted to credit to get by. When they couldn't make the minimum payments on their cards, Krista turned to friends for financial support. When their help ran dry, she turned to payday loans, which quickly got out of hand. She couldn't believe she was back in the same spot and just wouldn't go through bankruptcy again. But what choice did she have?

It's estimated that 15 percent or more of people who file for bankruptcy find themselves in the same predicament a few years later.[4] Although you're assigned a financial educator during the process (your bankruptcy trustee) and receive budgeting and financial literacy classes, the temptation of new credit eventually is often too strong for some people to resist.

THE SOLUTION?

You may not remember it, but there was a time not that long ago when you could only buy what you wanted with cash. No cash? No goods. It was that simple. Being lured by excess credit, even when it's a low-interest-rate line of credit, means profit for the banks and credit card companies, and possible peril for you. Understanding the true cost of debt is paramount. Overindulging today means there's less for tomorrow, not more. So how do you make lasting change?

Step #1: Visualize a Secure, Reasonable Financial Picture for Your Future Self

Krista needs to build a relationship with her future self. This requires some visualization. You, too, can try this technique. For the next week, spend ten minutes each morning asking yourself the following questions. The idea is to ingrain a strong, safe, reasonable financial vision for your future.

- How old will you be in ten years? Where would you like to be financially at that time?
- What work will you be doing? What will your family and social life look like?
- How much money will you need to do what you want?

By doing this every day for a few days, you're building a relationship with your future self in your mind. Once you have that clear in your own mind, it will be much easier to take smaller steps to make it happen.

Step #2: Don't Be Lured by Low Interest Rates

When interest rates are as low as they are right now and have been for years, it's all too tempting to take on new debt, like a mortgage, line of credit, or car loan. But if you don't have a sound plan to pay the money back, it's only going to sink you into a financial hole. Remember that no loan is ever free, and even a low rate of interest is a lot of money owed. Resist the urge to take money just because it's available at a low rate.

Step #3: Understand Lines of Credit

Usually, a line of credit is secured against your home's equity and used for renovations, an emergency account, or buying a car. As I write this, most major banks charge the prime rate of 2.45 percent plus 0.5 percent, and some credit unions charge only prime. Unlike a mortgage (which we covered in chapter 7), you don't have to pay the principal (original amount borrowed) in your monthly payments, only the interest. You can pay more if you'd like, but only the interest is due every month.

Let's look at an example:

- $50,000 line of credit
- 2.45 percent interest rate
- Minimum monthly payments = $102.08 per month, or $1,224.96 per year

You can see how that low monthly payment can tempt many people to use a line of credit for more than necessities, like rapidly ticking off items on their bucket list.

Since Krista wasn't a homeowner, the interest rate for her line of credit was significantly higher and got her in more trouble when she was paying it back (the higher interest rate meant an increased monthly cost to service her debt).

Step #4: Use a Line of Credit to Pay High-Interest-Rate Debt

Many people find overspending on a credit card is far too tempting and don't trust themselves to pay off their balance with a lower-rate loan or line of credit. Why? Because they think if they pay the entire amount off, they'll be enticed to rack it back up again.

When we look at Krista's credit cards, we can see how they were sinking her deeper into debt:

- Credit card #1: 28 percent interest, $3,600 balance, total interest paid per year: $1,008
- Credit card #2: 24.99 percent interest, $14,500 balance, total interest paid per year: $3,623.55
- Credit card #3: 12.99 percent interest, $2,500 balance, total interest paid per year: $324.75

You might be wondering how long it will take Krista to pay off her credit cards. Let's take a look and the total cost, assuming she makes only minimum payments on all of her accounts and doesn't add any new purchases:

- Credit card #1: Minimum payment of $108 a month would take around 5.5 years to pay off and cost $3,442 in interest.

- Credit card #2: Minimum payment of $435 a month would take around 4.8 years to pay off and cost $10,504 in interest.
- Credit card #3: Minimum payment of $75 a month would take around 3.5 years to pay off and cost $617 in interest.

Based on the above calculations, Krista will be paying $618 a month in minimum payments, but a whopping $14,563 in interest payments alone. That amount does not reflect other charges or the annual fees on all her cards, which add up to an additional $350 a year.

If Krista had paid off all her cards with her line of credit, she would have saved thousands of dollars each year. She had an unsecured line of credit for $30,000 with an interest rate of prime plus 3 percent for a total of 5.45 percent. Her total credit card debt was $20,600. If she paid it all off on her line of credit, that would equal $93.56 in minimum monthly payments or $1,122.72 per year. And if she got serious about paying attention to her debt and accelerating the payments, she could have paid just $393 per month and easily paid it off in five years. This would have been a significant difference compared to the $618 monthly minimum payment of her current scenario that will take longer than five years to pay off! And it would have only cost her a total of $2,982 in interest.

By simply using her line of credit to pay off her credit cards, she would have saved thousands of dollars that could have gone towards her emergency fund, savings, or even purchases for fun.

Step #5: Get a Credit Card with a Limit No Higher Than Your Monthly Budget

If you're tempted by a high-limit credit card or find yourself struggling to pay the balance off every month, you can lower the limit. Let's say your monthly spending is $1,000 and your limit is $1,000;

you simply won't be able to spend any further that month without hearing the word "declined." While that can sting, it's a great way to keep you on track if you often carry a balance on your credit cards.

How Much Do You Use?

In chapter two, we learned about credit card utilization—that's the percentage of available credit you use on your credit card. Having a high utilization can hurt your score, and it's easier to do if you have a low credit limit. However, if you're working to set new habits to not overspend on your credit card, it may be worth the possible credit score hit. That's a minor concern compared to getting in over your head. And you can always keep a line of credit with a high limit and ideally no balance to help stabilize your credit rating.

The great news is that it's really easy to switch to a lower-rate product just by calling your bank. You may not get all the perks and deals that you would with more costly reward card options, but if you're carrying a balance every month, resist the urge! You don't have the money to pay for more "perks" and "deals."

There are several low- or no-fee, low-interest-rate credit cards on the market and offered by every bank. If Krista had called up her bank to get out of her highest-balance credit card and have it transferred to a lower-rate one, she could have saved significant dollars (assuming she didn't have the option of using a line of credit). How would that have looked?

Remember her second credit card charged 24.99 percent interest, she had a balance of $14,500 on it, and she paid $3,623.55 a year in interest. If she could have lowered her interest rate to 12.99 percent, nearly half of what she was paying, she'd have slashed her annual interest cost to $1,883.52, for a savings of $1,740.03! That's a lot of money saved with one call. Not to mention these lower-interest-rate cards generally don't have an annual fee.

Let's look at the savings that call would have added up to for Krista:

- Her original annual fee of $150 a year equals $3,000 over twenty years.
- The lower-interest-rate savings of $1,740 a year equals $34,800 over twenty years.

You can see how retailers and banks want us to either ignore the cost of borrowing or to focus on the monthly cost, which can seem manageable. But when you take a long-lens view of the true cost of things such as annual fees and interest on a credit card balance where you're only making the minimum payment, the money saved could add more joy, security, and wealth in your life.

Let's Negotiate

As we covered in chapter 2, the caveat to negotiating with your creditor or getting them to work with you on an alternative payment plan or interest rate reduction is to contact them *well in advance* of missing a payment. Once you've missed a payment, it's far less likely that they'll be amenable to working with you.

Step #6: Avoid Over-Limit Fees

When you're nearly maxed out on your credit card, your provider may allow you to go over your limit—with a penalty.

Krista was at her limit each month on all of her cards. Since she was feeling stressed and overwhelmed by her debt, she never combed through her monthly statement and she failed to see these penalties. If she had taken a look and whipped open her calculator app, she would have realized that she was paying $87 a month in over-limit fees, or $1,044 a year.

Step #7: Get Organized to Keep Payments on Time

Missing a minimum payment on your credit card is even worse than being maxed out. It hurts your credit score and penalizes you with an increased interest rate temporarily.

Let's run the numbers. If you had a credit card with a balance of $5,000 at 19 percent interest, that would cost you $950 a year in interest. If you missed a payment or two and your rate was increased to 28 percent, you'd then pay $1,400 a year in interest. That's an additional $450 that's in your bank's pocket, not yours.

It can be easy to miss payments when you have a busy life, so don't leave your due dates to memory. If you carry credit card balances, make a list now of all your outstanding amounts, the interest rates you're paying, your minimum payments, and their due dates. As we covered in chapter 1, add these to your digital calendar along with a reminder at least one week in advance to nudge you to make these payments on time. Be sure to leave enough time for your payments to make it to your credit card company on or before the due date. You can also set up automatic payments with your bank or credit card company for extra reassurance.

Step #8: Determine Whether the Snowball or Avalanche Strategy Is Best for You

When you have several debts to pay like Krista, you have a couple of ways to tackle your payments. You can opt for the avalanche method, which means dealing with the highest-interest-rate debts first and the most savings for you. Alternatively, if this is too daunting, you might try the snowball method—paying your smallest debt first and then working up to the bigger ones. Neither method is absolutely right. It's whatever will get you motivated to flourish financially in the long run.

As for Krista, she opted for the snowball method. She needed some quick wins to build her financial self-esteem, so she paid off her overdue cell phone and electricity bills. Once those were ticked off her list, she tackled the credit card with the lowest balance. Then she moved on to payment arrangements with her dad and friends while she spread out payments on the rest of her debt owing. It felt good to build momentum, and she was surprised that paying off debt was actually exhilarating!

Step #9: Seek Help to Get Out of Financial Trouble

It's natural to feel ashamed of our money mistakes. However, our problems compound when we can't manage on our own and don't seek help. Think of it this way: Would you formulate a health-improvement plan before going to your doctor to see what's actually wrong with you? Probably not, and yet that is exactly what many people do when they find themselves in financial trouble that they barely comprehend.

When Krista first filed for bankruptcy, she did so without seeking opinions from various financial professionals so she could really understand the consequences, or pursuing other, possibly better solutions—such as calling up her creditors to negotiate manageable payments. If she had reached out for help at the first signs of trouble, she likely would have been able to avoid bankruptcy and would have reclaimed years of stress and lost sleep.

Credit Counsellors

The best place to find a qualified credit counsellor is at CreditCounsellingCanada.ca. The main consideration you must ask yourself is whether you can afford to make payments on your debt. If you can't, move on to the next section, on consumer proposals and bankruptcy.

Pros:

- Credit counselling organizations offer what's called a Debt Management Plan.
- They'll work with your creditors on your behalf to secure a payment arrangement.
- The arrangement obliges you to pay your debt and also helps you plan effectively.
- You have the support of the counsellor and organization. Many places offer free courses and additional support.

Cons:

- You might not be able to afford the arrangement they've worked out with your creditors.
- If you owe money to CRA, the debt cannot be negotiated by a credit counsellor.
- The arrangements with your creditors are voluntary and not legally binding. That means creditors could still contact you.
- The process will affect your credit score negatively.

- There may be fees for working with credit counsellors. Ask about up-front fees, consultation fees, and costs associated with your Debt Management Plan.

Once you've shopped around for a non-profit credit counsellor, you'll also want to carefully review the Debt Management Plan to ensure that all your debts and arrangements have been agreed to by your creditors. Make sure you stay involved in the process and understand the ins and outs. Always take time to read the fine print and ask questions. Shop around if you're not getting clear answers.

Consumer proposals (CP) versus bankruptcy

The main difference between a consumer proposal and bankruptcy is the monthly payment you'll have to make to your creditors.

A CP is a settlement of your debt that is legally binding, and no creditor can demand more than the amount you've settled on. You'll need an insolvency trustee to approach your lenders on your behalf. Once your CP is filed, all garnishes stop.

The big plus with CPs is that you get to keep your assets, including your home, but each province is different. With bankruptcy, you don't get to keep your assets.

A CP gets rid of:

- credit card debt
- payday loans
- bank loans
- tax debt
- certain student loan debt
- calls from your creditors

You must show that you have income sufficient to pay your debts and are insolvent (have stopped paying your debts). CPs address debts that range from $1,000 to $250,000. The process is much less complicated than bankruptcy and generally costs less as well. Another plus of a CP over bankruptcy is that the latter can hinder your ability to obtain some professional designations, business licenses, and even jobs (especially in the financial industry).

As you will see from the graphic on the next page, CPs cost the least because an insolvency trustee can negotiate your debt and interest down with your creditors. In the end, they reap the most benefits in terms of the cost to the consumer. The next best option is working with a credit counsellor, but the cost is still considerably higher as credit counsellors can't negotiate a consumer's debt down.

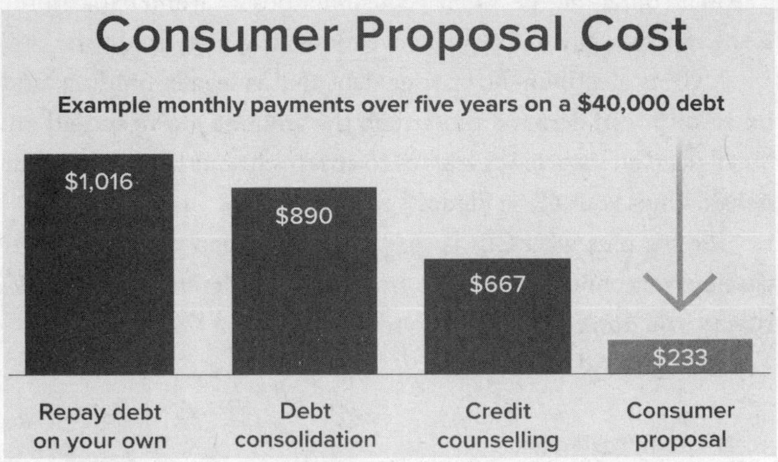

When deciding which process is right for you, an insolvency trustee will look at your income, assets, total debt, and cost associated with each process. There's no right solution for everyone, so you need to get several professional opinions in writing.

WHERE IS SHE NOW?

When Krista found herself in financial trouble a second time, her close friends and family told her to file for bankruptcy again. But she just couldn't this time. It was a wake-up call for her to finally get her finances figured out.

She met with a non-profit credit counsellor who put a Debt Management Plan in place. Her credit counsellor was able to negotiate lower interest rates and payments for some of her debts. She had five years to pay off her debt under this plan, but she was super motivated to get it paid even sooner.

Krista never believed in small gains until she tried them. Her credit counsellor gave her some tips for getting debt-free sooner, such as making her coffee and lunch at home. She also took a six-month spending break on wants and practiced gratitude for the things she had. With the extra savings she found each month, she started an emergency fund. She checked her bank app each month, and while the balance was seemingly insignificant in the early days, at the end of the year, she had to pinch herself. It was working.

When the five years were up, Krista had met her goal. Her Debt Management Plan was complete. She was solvent and debt-free for the first time in her adult life. She promised herself she'd never go back to her old ways.

Krista still indulges from time to time but has a clear plan for doing so, and she never uses credit other than to pay for her groceries and gas and then immediately pays her card off as soon as she gets home. This practice has skyrocketed her credit score in the past year from 595 to a decent 720.

Paying attention to her finances finally feels easy and fun. Krista has actually started saving! She wishes she had learned these lessons sooner, but she's proud of herself for owning her past mistakes and for committing to never repeating them again.

Big Spending, Big Problems

Josephine grew up as a typical Gen X-er latchkey kid. Her mom and dad split when she was young, and with her mom working overtime to make ends meet, most days she arrived home to cook her own dinner and entertain herself. Josephine took risks at school and in her playtime to relieve boredom and push her limits. With no parental supervision, she could skip school and do as she pleased.

This adventurous and often hazardous spirit followed her into adulthood. She was impulsive with money and never hesitated to make a decision on the spot. But these choices often came with a cost—and much regret.

When her mom got sick with cancer, Josephine was stressed and needed a distraction. She decided to renovate her home, and of course she had to redecorate, too! Instead of taking her time refurnishing her refreshed digs, she went on shopping sprees because she wanted the house put back together immediately. Not surprisingly, after a few months, her new stuff didn't excite her any longer. She was back to worrying about her mother's health all the time—and now she had to worry about all the money she'd just blown, too.

Sadly, not long after the reno and redecorating were complete, Josephine's mother died. Josephine was totally heartbroken. Her mom had only ever worked minimum-wage positions and struggled financially her entire life. To Josephine's great surprise, she found out that her mom had purchased a life insurance policy decades ago, and when she died, Josephine received $100,000 tax-free. It was an emotionally charged gift that was very welcome but also made Josephine sad—her mom was giving her a windfall that she had never got to enjoy in her own life.

Josephine made quick use of the funds. Her mom's voice echoed in her head: "You can only make money if you have money." Now that she had some, she tried her hand at day-trading, buying $10,000 in cryptocurrencies.

Next, she decided to sell her newly renovated home and buy something even better. The new house was worth only $150,000 more than her own, so she bought it before she sold her first house, feeling pretty secure that her first home would sell for top dollar.

What do you think happened? You can probably guess: things didn't work out so well for Josephine. Let's have a look at how her overconfidence in the value of her own home and her emotional spending spree after the loss of her mother led to some very costly mistakes.

WHERE SHE WENT WRONG

Misstep #1: Engaging in Emotional Spending Sprees

Suffering the death of a loved one can often trigger emotional behaviour, especially when it comes to money. It could happen to you as it did with Josephine. The largest transfer of wealth in history is happening right now. It's estimated that more than $723 billion in Canadian assets will be transferred to boomers and Gen X-ers over the next decade from their parents.[1] It's easy to think of this "free money" as a welcome gift, but often, when it's the result of the death of a loved one, the influx of cash sometimes gets spent a bit too impulsively. This might be due to mismanagement or a lack of financial literacy, but often there's another reason, too: when a windfall occurs because of a death, feelings of loss are involved. And sometimes, we want to heal that pain the wrong way—through irrational spending.

Of course, there are other kinds of "found money" besides inheritances. Sometimes a windfall comes as a tax refund (which is really your money returned to you by the government, without interest), a bonus from your workplace, or a new credit limit increase (which, of course, isn't actually found money at all but potential debt!). These "windfalls" can trigger erratic spending that most of us would normally never engage in with our regular paycheques.

Misstep #2: Being Overconfident in Real Estate

Think about your driving skills for a moment. Do you believe you're better than most other drivers on the road? If you answered yes, you're in the company of 93 percent of us. But you can see that the math is flawed. How can we all be above average? We indulge in these overconfidence biases all the time. We make decisions consciously and subconsciously (or with intuition). When you're an expert with decades of experience in something, trusting your gut can be wise. But when you're a novice, not trusting your feelings is a smarter move. If you question this, look up brilliant investors such as Bill Gates, who wasted money on the Segway. There are many great minds who are experts in their respective fields, but when it comes to trusting their guts on a new idea, they can get it wrong. The Segway, which Bill Gates and many others believed would revolutionize walking and transportation, was a flop. This goes to show you: even brilliant minds don't get things right all the time.

Josephine was overconfident about the value of her home. Just because she'd renovated it did not mean it was worth more. She'd knocked out two bedrooms to make one large master bedroom. She'd added a pool and hot tub and opted for high-end furnishings and finishes in a midmarket neighbourhood. This meant she had fewer potential buyers . . . and even fewer offers once she needed to sell.

Studies reveal that we value things differently depending on whether they belong to us or not. For example, we highly value what is ours and discount what others are selling. When we put effort into something, we estimate its worth as much more valuable because of our sweat equity.

Misstep #3: Falling for a "Recency Bias"

Recency bias occurs when, because of a surge in a market, we believe that surge will continue. From an investment perspective, recency bias can cause people to buy high and sell low, investing during a frenzy of market activity and unloading in a panic.

A few days after Josephine received the life insurance proceeds cheque, she was watching the evening news about skyrocketing returns on Bitcoin and this new digital mode of currency taking the world by storm. She immediately decided to open up several accounts, pour in $10,000, and gamble on a few cryptocurrencies that she knew very little about. She invested with a fraudulent offering and lost all of that money. Her recency bias—alongside poor research and lack of information—cost her quite a bit of money.

THE SOLUTION?

Josephine can reassess her illogical spending and investing to get herself back on track. If you see yourself making some of the same financial decisions as Josephine, here's how you can open your eyes to better decision-making in the future.

Step #1: View Money Rationally

All money in your hands is your money. Found money shouldn't be spent or viewed more impulsively than earned money. Many people see their RRSP or child's RESP as a sacred investment not to be gambled, and therefore, they may take too few risks with it over time and leave growth opportunities on the table. In contrast, people can be impetuous with their TFSA withdrawals, which can be accessed without the same repercussions as RRSP withdrawals. Remember: it's all money, and none of it should be used without discretion and forethought.

When it comes to our spending, many of us have moments of irrational thinking. Let's take two scenarios. Here's the first: You're in the market for a new lamp. You've even saved up for it. You find the perfect one at $50 and are incredibly happy with the price.

Just before you pay, your friend walks into the store and tells you that the exact same lamp is on sale for $25 about two blocks away. My question to you is, do you go to the other store? Some people wouldn't, even though the 50 percent savings are incredible!

Here's the second scenario: You're shopping for a big-screen TV. You've finally narrowed it down to the perfect one. The price is $1,250. Your friend walks into the store and tells you the exact TV is on sale at a store about two blocks away for $25 less. Do you go?

When I pose this question to audiences, there's often lots of grumbling. Some shout yes, others no. But here's the rub—in either of these scenarios, you can save the same amount: $25. If you'd make the effort to save $25 when it represents a larger percentage, why wouldn't you make the same effort when the percentage is smaller? After all, it's the same amount of money!

Retailers trick us with the dollar-versus-percentage conundrum all the time. They might say something is only $1 a day so we don't get the sticker shock of $365 for an annual charge. I fall prey to the percentage-versus-dollar analysis all the time, but less so now that my eyes are open to the cost of saying yes to every so-called bargain waved before my eyes.

Recently, my husband was under the weather and asked me to do the grocery shopping (which I never do as I'm usually travelling for work). He had ice cream on the list, and since I don't eat it often, I don't know the prices well. As I got to the freezer and saw the tiny and expensive container of coffee Häagen-Dazs he'd requested, I searched for an item that offered better value. My husband takes great pride in being a frugal shopper (unlike me), so I thought I'd do him proud by being the same way.

I finally decided on the large tub of vanilla ice cream—ten times the size of the coffee Häagen-Dazs and nearly half the price. Upon returning home and unpacking the groceries, I beamed with pride as I presented the bargain. My husband shook his head.

"More isn't always more, you know," he said. "Sometimes more is less." He then schooled me on the fact that I'd bought a poor facsimile of ice cream, not the real thing at all—and I'd bought way more than he could ever eat.

He eyed my designer purse, which sat beside the giant tub of ice cream. "You bought that for a lot of money because it gives you pleasure. Can't we spend a few dollars more to get me quality ice cream?"

He had a point. This is a classic case of looking at the percentage instead of the dollars. I saw a 50 percent savings for my husband's treat, but the difference was only about $3 or $4 overall, and I bought him something that he wasn't going to eat. The point? If you're going to invest in a small item for pure pleasure, don't let a few dollars hold you back!

Step #2: Know When a Small Percentage Adds Up

While my ice-cream error shows money can be poorly saved, there are instances when a small percentage gain actually amounts to big dollars. One such instance is with mortgage rates. When Josephine bought her new home, she had to get a mortgage, and she took whatever rate was offered. If she'd shopped around, she could have saved about 1 percent, maybe more. That doesn't sound like much, but it really is when a large sum of money is amortized over a long period of time.

With interest rates currently so incredibly low, many people fail to negotiate further with their lender. But it's never been easier to shop the competition online and then arm yourself with special rates and price breaks to see how much you can reduce your rate. A

1 percent difference or even less on a large sum could cost you tens if not hundreds of thousands of dollars over your lifetime.

The overall message here: don't ignore percentages when negotiating your mortgage or investment fees with your financial advisor.

Step #3: Take a Spending Break When Emotions Are High

Receiving an inheritance, tax refund, or bonus can activate a spending reflex. The best course of action when you know your feelings are triggered is to take a decision breather. Put the money in a bank account that you don't see all the time for safekeeping. (You can even hide your online bank accounts, so they don't show up when you log in.) Give yourself a few weeks or months of space before deciding what to do with the windfall. This way, some of the instant emotional triggers will wear off and you'll be less likely to make a poor decision.

Step #4: Limit Big Purchases Over Time

Josephine went from a huge home renovation to selling her home all in the space of a year. And her renos were not planned with selling in mind, so the bottom-line losses were significant. Now that she's in her new home, guess what she's thinking? That's right: she's got the reno bug and is considering remodelling her kitchen.

Here's the thing: she made this mistake before and it cost her. In a year's time, she might regret putting in that new kitchen. Instead of rushing ahead and filling her life with projects, she needs to start capping her big spends every year.

When we pile up major decisions, we fail to see that there are many underlying yet significant considerations that need to be weighed individually. If we don't, we might fall prey to making a number of wrong moves.

Step #5: Spread Out Purchases for Maximum Enjoyment

Much research has been done on spending and our happiness. Even lottery winners return to the same mood they were once in just a short six months after winning a huge amount of money. Think buying a luxury car or bag will end your doldrums? For a while, maybe, but not forever.

Spreading out your purchases has been shown to create more satisfaction over the long term.[2] Josephine's always in a rush to get her decorating done, but she would have found much more pleasure and enjoyment in buying an item or two at a time. Not only could she maximize her shopping pleasure, but the spacing of items would allow her to savour them individually as she added them to her home. You'll likely enjoy one new item as much as several, so try spreading purchases out over a few weeks or months. This goes for gifts for others, too.

Step #6: Be Mindful of the Diderot Effect

French philosopher Denis Diderot lived in poverty most of his life, but that all changed in the late 1700s. Catherine the Great purchased his library of encyclopedias for what is estimated to be worth around $50,000 in today's dollars. So, what was Diderot to do with his newfound wealth? What any gentleman of that era would have done: splurge on a scarlet robe. The problem was that as he looked around at his home, everything paled in comparison to his new garment. He ordered a lavish rug from Damascus, sculptures, modern furniture, and more. You get the idea. His innocent new robe levelled up his expectations and measure of satisfaction with the things in his home.

When Josephine set out to only renovate her kitchen (the first time!), it had a domino effect. She then had to renovate everything. There's nothing wrong with levelling up, just be sure it doesn't come at a cost that you cannot bear.

Here are some common scenarios where one purchase triggers more spending:

- You get invited to play a game of golf with friends. You buy a new outfit to fit in. Will you stop yourself there, or are you now going to buy golf clubs and shoes, too, before you even know if you like the game?
- You replace a worn-out chair the cat scratched to oblivion. The new, stylish piece arrives, but now everything else in the room looks shabby by comparison. Uh-oh: this is how the splurging on furniture begins.
- You buy a new gaming console for your teenager, who now claims they need hundreds of dollars in new games.

Once you become aware of the Diderot effect, you can stop it in its tracks. Resist the urge to buy everything just because you spent on one item.

Step #7: Renovate Smartly

In 2019, Canadians spent more than $80 billion on home renovations.[3] You likely won't be surprised that $61.2 billion of that spending was allocated to upgrades, not necessity repairs. And how are people generally paying for their shiny, upgraded homes? The estimate is that $14 billion of what was spent was secured via financing, through home equity lines of credit and other debts.[4]

Most experts agree that the two rooms in your home that will yield you the maximum return for your investment are your kitchen and bathroom—not a pool and hot tub, as Josephine opted for.

What's Worth Renovating?

Here's a snapshot of purchases that net you the best return on investment (ROI) when it comes time to sell your property:

- Paint
- Windows
- Roof
- Waterproofing your foundation
- Doors and hardware
- Kitchens
- Bathrooms
- Flooring[5]

Step #8: Understand Alternative Investments and Their Risks

In chapter 6, you learned about diversification and the traditional investments available to you, such as GICs, stocks, bonds, mutual funds, and ETFs. But there are other investments that fall into the category of alternative investments. "Alternative investments" refers loosely to nonconventional assets such as wine, art, private companies, and more.

Tell Me More

Here are some examples of alternative investments:

Real estate

- You can buy real estate to rent out or simply flip for a potential profit. If you do it yourself, there's considerable time and expertise involved in this investment, as well as costs. If you hire a management firm to handle your property for you, you'll have to weigh its costs and how much they will eat into your profit.
- With a real estate investment trust (REIT), you can gain exposure to commercial and residential real estate markets without having to worry about the buying, selling, or management of properties. Think of a REIT as a mutual fund or ETF that invests in real estate. And there are also private REITs and limited partnerships as well. They're traded on an exchange and can be bought and sold more easily than owning an individual property.

Private equity

- Large players like pension funds often invest in private equity, and it usually involves a high minimum investment. With this strategy, you invest in the equity of a private corporation that doesn't trade on a stock exchange like a publicly traded company. There may be an illiquidity premium that makes the private company cheaper to buy than a public company with the same profitability. But it's more difficult to value a private company than a public company that gets valued every day by the buyers and sellers in the stock market. The thing with a private company investment is you may have to be in it for the long run, but there may be more upside potential. It's illiquid, and thus you may earn a higher return, but with a more variable upside or downside outcome.

- There are a number of investment companies offering lower entry into investments in the private equity space or within a mutual fund. They'll likely grow in popularity as they seek to attract midmarket investors. Make sure to do your due diligence if investing.

Cryptocurrencies

- Like Josephine, you've no doubt heard of Bitcoin and other popular digital currencies. They allow you to tap into forms of spending that aren't reliant on traceable cash such as legal tender, debit, or credit. Some say these are a crazy fad and other experts maintain they're here to stay. Think of a cryptocurrency as a medium of exchange that is independent of a central bank (like the Bank of Canada, for example). The value is stored in a ledger in a decentralized database and fluctuates wildly. Cryptocurrencies are considered highly unstable compared to normal currency (money).
- The touted benefits are that it's virtually impossible to double-spend or counterfeit cryptocurrency. However, as we've

learned from Josephine, it's best to know what you're investing in, as it's easy to fall victim to fraudsters or to currency fluctuations.

There are some pros to alternative investments. First, they may provide more diversification to decrease your overall portfolio risk. Also, they often offer higher rates of return. Some alternative investments may help you to invest in an asset class you couldn't otherwise own directly (like infrastructure, private equity, or even certain types of real estate).

But you can't consider the pros without the cons. One con of alternative investments is that you need to be an accredited or eligible investor. That means you may have to have a certain level of income or net worth. Private-market investment rules differ by province. The complex strategies mean you have to be a sophisticated investor to understand them. Additionally, holdings are sometimes hard to liquidate, the fees can be quite high, and the terms can be very difficult to understand. If you're thinking of alternative investments, make sure you get an experienced, independent third-party evaluation from a fee-based Certified Financial Planner or a Chartered Professional Accountant.

WHERE IS SHE NOW?

Josephine, always itching for a new adventure, couldn't resist accepting a job offer a couple of provinces away. Actually, she was looking for any excuse to sell her home—yes, the one she moved into less than a year ago! This move meant a fresh start. But for once, Josephine actually did her research and understood the financial variables before taking the plunge.

Her new house was much more marketable than her last one. She met with several Realtors for a consensus on its value and was delighted to learn it had already appreciated in a year. This time, she decided to sell first so she knew how much she could spend in the new city she was moving to, where house values were considerably lower. Her house sold for top dollar in just fifteen days.

Josephine took it slow when deciding on her new home. She had a closing date months away to allow herself the time to consider her next steps prudently. She sat down with her banker and a Certified Financial Planner to determine whether she should rent in her new city and, if so, what the costs would be for breaking her mortgage term. She used her credit card reward points to fly out to shop the market in advance. In the past, she would have made a decision impulsively on the internet. After meeting with a leasing agent and Realtor there, she researched the best neighbourhoods and proximity to her new job. In the end, she bought a condo in her new city. Though it was a hefty cost to break her mortgage, the cost of the condo was significantly lower than the price her home had sold for. This meant money in the bank—and savings for a new life in a new place.

For once, Josephine didn't blow the windfall on new stuff. Instead, she sold her furniture in her current house because it would have cost a fortune to move it. She decided she would furnish her new place piece by piece, turning first to Kijiji and Facebook Marketplace rather than to high-end furniture stores.

Josephine is now happily settled into her condo. She has a couch and some nice chairs, which she refinished herself. She still needs a credenza and a couple of dressers, but for now, she's managing. It feels good to have a nest egg in her bank account, and she's decided not to touch it for at least two months. First, she needs to get to know the area and to feel comfortable in her job. Once all the high emotions settle, then she'll make a plan for what to do next. One thing's for sure—she will *not* be remodelling the kitchen.

11

Where Are You Now?

Some final parting thoughts . . .

My brother was a huge fan of *Star Wars* growing up. When he was young, he'd often repeat the sage wisdom of Yoda: "Do or do not, there is no try."

Wherever you are on your financial journey, remember that it's never too late to act. Broke girls get stuck in a rut of repeating the same financial errors over and over or doing nothing at all. The women I've known who are the most financially healthy make finances a daily priority. Some days, paying attention to your money situation will be fun and rewarding; other days, it will feel like the cheque just bounced. Either way, it's the doing that matters. Passivity is not an option.

I'd also like to say that wherever you are on your financial path, like it or not, money's right there with you. You can't escape it. I've known people who believed they had "won" at the financial game, who thought they never had to think about money ever again. Guess what? Many of them had financial setbacks that made them realize the importance of always being attuned to their finances. The good news is that even if you do experience a financial loss, maybe due to a layoff at work, divorce, or business failure, while it will be a shock, the best thing to do is to stay savvy and informed about your financial prospects. It is possible to turn a financial frown upside down. I've seen it over and over, with people from all walks of life in all kinds of financial situations.

Rich girls know that money is for life. You can't just decide to remain uninformed and hope for the best. Rich girls have a clear sense that money isn't everything that matters, that financial awareness is important but true prosperity comes from much more than money alone. Rich girls also know that their wealth is the key to their independence, not only for themselves, but for their dependents, too. Rich girls spend and save intelligently, read the fine print, and know how to talk money. But they also know how to splurge every once in a while, on themselves and on the things that matter most.

Our journey on these pages has come to an end, but our relationship has not. I'd love to hear from you about your money joys and struggles, your scratches and slivers along the way, your little financial successes and your big triumphs, too! Reach out on Twitter @kelleykeehn or on Instagram @kelleykeehnbiz, or email me at info@kelleykeehn.com.

Here's to your prosperity!

Kelley Keehn

Glossary

amortization: This is how long you have to pay off your mortgage. Think of it as the gradual time it takes to pay back a big debt. In Canada, you can have a mortgage amortization of up to twenty-five years.

asset: An investment that you own in your name and hope will increase in value over time, such as a house, piece of art, or collector car.

beneficiary: The person whom you name to inherit your money or other assets when you pass away.

blue-chip stock: This is a stock with a company that typically has a large market capitalization, an exceptional reputation, and many years of success in the business world.

bond: As an investor, when you own a bond, you're *owed* money. The interest is fixed and is considered income that you're paid annually or more frequently, which is why this asset class is often referred to as *fixed income*.

cash: A cash asset is an investment that is easily accessible but for which you get a meagre return in interest because current interest rates are very low.

Certified Financial Planner (CFP): A professional in the personal finance industry certified with the most widely recognized financial planning designation in Canada. They provide financial planning strategies and solutions and work with you to create a financial plan that suits your unique situation—no matter how big or small the problem.

collections account: If you have something "in collections," a debt is outstanding and grossly overdue—it usually takes ninety days or more for your lender to write off a debt and send it to a collection agency to try to recoup the funds.

credit score: Your credit score can range from 300 to 900. While high scores are the most favourable, only an estimated 5 percent of Canadians have a score over 850, and it's the range that matters, not the actual number. A credit report will indicate where your score stands in the following ranges: Poor, Fair, Good, Very Good, and Excellent.

defined contribution plan: A pension plan in which you know what you and your employer are contributing, but there is no set amount you'll have at retirement.

dividend: A financial bonus for investing in a public company (when you buy a preferred share).

emergency fund: A fully funded emergency account, which should contain three to six months of your household income. If you're self-employed, have a highly specialized job, or work in an unstable industry, an emergency fund should cover as much as one year of your household income.

garnish: To seize wages or other funds from someone who has not paid a debt. When you've fallen behind on your debt payments, a creditor can take money directly from your bank account or your employment payments.

gross income: Total income before the deduction of any costs. More commonly, gross income refers to income before tax deductions.

group registered retirement savings plan (group RRSP): A savings plan to which you contribute payments, administered by your employer. These are the most popular with employers today.

hard credit inquiry: These inquiries result from actively seeking credit and can affect your credit score. If you apply for a new car loan, credit card, or even cell phone, you agree to have a credit check performed, which will appear on your credit report as a hard inquiry.

Home Buyers' Plan (HBP): This is a provision that allows you to take money out of your RRSP without paying tax if you're a first-time home buyer. You can withdraw up to $35,000 from your plan in a calendar year. You have to start making payments back to your RRSP in the second year and generally have fifteen years to pay yourself back, but you can do so at any time. You will be taxed on your withdrawal if you don't comply with the Government of Canada's rules.

line of credit: A line of credit is like a credit card with no card attached to it and offers a much better interest rate, and it doesn't cost you anything unless you use it.

liquidity: Your investments are liquid when you can sell the assets quickly and get your money back when you need it. A house, real estate, and art are all examples of investments that aren't very liquid because they take time to sell.

mortgage: A long-term loan against your house provided by a bank or lender. A mortgage requires you to make payments over a longer period, between ten and twenty-five years.

mutual fund: A pool of investments that includes the professional services of a mutual fund manager. There are thousands of mutual funds available in the Canadian marketplace, which range in level of risk and return opportunities.

net income: Total income after taxes are deducted. It's what you have left in your bank before paying any expenses.

net worth statement: A calculation that balances out how much you own and how much you owe to give you a full picture of your financial health. The exercise of calculating your net worth encourages you to dig through your assets and debts.

non-profit credit counsellor: A professional in the personal finance industry who can offer an initial financial assessment at no cost to you, and can provide options for getting out of debt after reviewing your income, expenses, credit standing, assets, and debts.

power of attorney (POA): A document that designates someone who can act on your behalf while you're alive. After you pass away, their power ceases, and your executor steps in to help handle your estate. They can be the same person, but they don't have to be.

registered education savings plan (RESP): A registered savings plan that you set up to save for your child's education. There are no tax deductions, and there is a lifetime contribution limit of $50,000 per child in your household. The big plus is the government grant, which grows tax-deferred.

registered retirement savings plan (RRSP): A retirement savings plan that you establish and contribute to, and the money in the plan grows tax-deferred—you won't pay any tax until you start withdrawing money, which usually happens at retirement.

soft credit inquiry: These credit inquiries do not count against your score but may still appear on your report. They result from checking your report or a company's checking your credit as part of a background check. You can check your credit report as often as you like without its affecting your score.

stock: You can purchase shares—or equity—to have partial ownership in a company in the form of stock. If the company does well, you do well, but if the company tanks or goes bankrupt, you could lose everything.

tax-free savings account (TFSA): When you have money in a TFSA, your money is truly tax-free: it can grow and be withdrawn tax-free. A TFSA, like an RRSP or an RESP, is a garage shielding your car from taxation and can contain multiple investments.

Acknowledgements

A very special thanks to Jason Heath, a fee-only financial planner with Objective Financial Partners, for lending his expertise to this book.

To Nita Pronovost, my incredible editor at Simon & Schuster Canada—when I told my friend David Chilton (a.k.a. the Wealthy Barber) about who my publisher was for this and my last book, he exclaimed that I must get you as my editor because you're the best in the world. He was right! This book is as much your creation as mine, and I thank you for your brilliant oversight on this project. And for coming up with the idea over a glass of wine at the Four Seasons Toronto.

To Karen Silva, thank you for your savvy editing skills and excitement during every step of the publication of this book. You and Nita allowed me to have the confidence to just write, knowing your red pen would make the content palatable and even pop for our readers. And to Kevin Hanson, head of Simon & Schuster Canada: as a businesswoman and an author who self-published her first book, I know how incredibly lucky I am to have had this title chosen as one of your publications. Thank you also to Felicia Quon, Adria Iwastiak, David Millar, Mackenzie Croft, Rebecca Snoddon, Jasmine Elliott, and Aja Pollock for your help getting the book into readers' hands. It's an author's dream to work with such a dynamic and professional team of passionate fellow literature lovers.

Thank you to Rachel Wood for bringing her husband to our cocktail meeting in Vancouver so many years ago. And to Brian Wood, who became my literary agent over a strong scotch that afternoon. I didn't think I had another book in me, but you knew otherwise. If it weren't for your belief in my mission to help Canadians to feel good about money and your expertise, this book would have never been born.

Eternal gratitude to my angel and hero, Kathleen Keehn. If I had simply listened to your financial advice over the years, I wouldn't have had to write so many books on the subject. You've always taught me generosity, especially when one seemingly has nothing to give. No project in my life ever starts or ends without your undying love and enthusiasm. To echo the words of Abraham Lincoln, all that I am or ever hope to be, I owe to my mother.

No book in my life would have ever been written without the encouragement of my husband, Wyatt Cavanaugh. He first planted the seeds in my doubting mind sixteen years ago, and it's only with his vision and love that this undertaking was even a possibility. I'm so lucky to have his support in life and brilliant mind to bounce every book idea and project off.

To my mentors Marilyn Denis and David Chilton: your friendship and guidance over the years has been incredibly valuable to me and has benefited this book immensely.

Thank you to those who lent their time and expertise to this project: Krista Scaldwell, Doug Hoyes, Lucie Tedesco, and Kimberly Ney.

Thank you to the Buffalo Mountain Lodge and the phenomenal staff who took great care of me during my many, many solo writing retreats at their gorgeous cabins atop Tunnel Mountain.

Heartfelt thanks to my general manager, Miroki Tong. Not only for enriching this book, but for brilliantly handling our business while I was MIA working on this manuscript. I'm beyond appreciative of your dedication to and passion for this project as well as lifting up women financially.

To my loving family: my brothers, Randy and David; my sister-in-law, Elaine; my nieces and nephew, Dr. Amelia Keehn, Dr. Alysha Keehn, Jude, and Adam; and my dear friend Carl. I thank you for your patience and acceptance of my many missed family appearances, and for your understanding, passion for my work, and much-needed love and support.

Last but never least, thank you to my cats Niles and Frasier for your welcome interruptions during my writing process. Your unconditional love and playtime made completing this more fun.

Notes

Introduction

1 AAN team, "Women Hold 40% of Global Wealth—Credit Suisse Research Institute," Asia Advisers Network, October 30, 2018, www.asiaadvisersnetwork.com/Article?aid=44659.

2 "Canadian Women Control Financial Assets of $2.2T, CIBC Says," CBC.ca, March 4, 2019, www.cbc.ca/news/business/cibc-study-women-wealth-1.5039784.

3 Ryan Gorman, "Women Now Control More Than Half of US Personal Wealth, Which 'Will Only Increase in Years to Come,'" *Business Insider*, April 7, 2015, www.businessinsider.com/personal-finance/women-now-control-more-than-half-of-us-personal-wealth-2015-4.

4 Cassie Werber, "Wealthy Millennial Women Are More Likely to Defer to Their Husbands on Investing," *Quartz*, updated March 19, 2019, qz.com/work/1573457.

5 Ibid.

6 Allison Sadlier, "Two-thirds of Women Whose Partners Are the Primary Breadwinners Say They Feel Trapped," SWNSdigital

.com, February 4, 2020, swnsdigital.com/2020/02/two-thirds-of-women-whose-partners-are-the-primary-breadwinners-say-they-feel-trapped.

1. The Hidden Price of an Expensive Life

1 John Shmuel, "When It Comes to Financial Literacy, Canadians Really Overestimate Their Knowledge," LowestRates.ca, June 27, 2017, www.lowestrates.ca/blog/finance/when-it-comes-financial-literacy-canadians-really-overestimate-their-knowledge.

2 Marcel Schwantes, "Science Says Only 8 Percent of People Actually Achieve Their Goals. Here Are 7 Things They Do Differently," *Inc.*, May 21, 2021, www.inc.com/marcel-schwantes/science-says-only-8-percent-of-people-actually-achieve-their-goals-here-are-7-things-they-do-differently.html.

2. Honey, It's *My* Money—Taking Back Financial Control

1 "Own Your Worth 2020," UBS, accessed June 16, 2021, advisors.ubs.com/patricia.kelley/mediahandler/media/323256/own-your-worth-report-2020.pdf.

2 Ibid.

3 "Pet Care Costs," ASPCA, accessed June 16, 2021, www.aspca.org/sites/default/files/pet_care_costs.pdf.

4 "Costs of Dog Ownership," American Kennel Club, accessed June 16, 2021, images.akc.org/pdf/press_center/costs_of_dog_ownership.pdf.

5 Eric Barker, "32 Ways to Quickly and Easily Improve Your Life," *Business Insider*, July 13, 2021, www.businessinsider.com/32-ways-to-quickly-and-easily-improve-your-life-2012-7.

6 FP Canada, "The Value of Financial Planning," Financial Planning for Canadians, accessed June 16, 2021, www.financialplanningforcanadians.ca/financial-planning/benefits-of-financial-planning.

3. She Who Talks Money, Earns Money

1 Amy Morin, "Workplace Strengths: Science Explains What Men Do Best Vs. What Women Do Best," *Inc.*, August 29, 2016, www.inc.com/amy-morin/mens-business-strengths-vs-womens-business-strengths-science-reveals-there-are-c.html.

2 Ibid.

3 Michael J. O'Brien, "What Do Today's Job Candidates Really Want?" Human Resource Executive, July 23, 2019, hrexecutive.com/what-do-todays-candidates-really-want.

4 Ibid.

5 Alison Doyle, "How Often Do People Change Jobs During a Lifetime?," The Balance Careers, June 15, 2020, www.thebalancecareers.com/how-often-do-people-change-jobs-2060467.

6 Sarah Niedoba, "Half of Canadian Women Regularly Fantasize About Quitting Their Jobs," *Canadian Business*, January 11, 2017, www.canadianbusiness.com/innovation/chatelaine-this-is-40ish-women-careers-quitting-fantasies.

7 Cameron Keng, "Employees Who Stay in Companies Longer Than Two Years Get Paid 50% Less," *Forbes*, June 22, 2014, www.forbes.com/sites/cameronkeng/2014/06/22/employees-that-stay-in-companies-longer-than-2-years-get-paid-50-less.

8 Tara Sophia Mohr, "Why Women Don't Apply for Jobs Unless They're 100% Qualified," *Harvard Business Review*, August 25, 2014, hbr.org/2014/08/why-women-dont-apply-for-jobs-unless-theyre-100-qualified.

4. I Never Said "I Do" to Your Debt

1 "Common Law Marriage in Ontario," Feldstein Family Law Group PC, accessed June 17, 2021, www.separation.ca/family-law/common-law.

2 Elizabeth Palmieri, "Video: What Does a University Education Cost in Canada?," *Maclean's*, November 8, 2017, www.macleans.ca/education/uniandcollege/what-does-a-university-education-cost-in-canada.

3 Ibid.

4 "Canadian MBC Tuition Fees," Canadian-Universities.net, accessed June 17, 2021, www.canadian-universities.net/MBA/MBA_Tuition_Canada.html.

5 "Student Debt Crisis—A Generation Buried in Student Debt," Hoyes, Michalos & Associates Inc., accessed June 17, 2021, www.hoyes.com/press/joe-debtor/the-student-debtor.

6 Azzura Lalani, "With More Than $5 Million Going Unclaimed Each Year, Students Advised to Apply to as Many as They Can," *London Free Press*, May 27, 2015, lfpress.com/2015/05/27/with-more-than-5-million-going-unclaimed-each-year-students-advised-to-apply-to-as-many-as-they-can.

7 *Insurance Journal* staff, "Parents Ready to Make Sacrifices to Help Adult Children Buy Homes," Insurance Portal, July 23, 2019, insurance-portal.ca/article/parents-ready-to-make-sacrifices-to-help-adult-children-buy-homes.

8 Elizabeth O'Brien, "Parents Are Giving Their Kids an Average of $39,000 to Buy a Home—and It Could Jeopardize Their Own Retirement," Money.com, May 17, 2019, money.com/parents-adult-children-house-down-payments-retirement.

9 Sean Simpson, "Majority (56%) of Canadian Parents Not Taking Advantage of RESP Grants," Ipsos, August 29, 2017, www.ipsos.com/en-ca/news-polls/canada-parents-RESP-knowledge-first-financial.

10 Ashley Turner, "The 'Bizarre' Money Secret Many Americans Keep—Even from Their Spouse," CNBC.com, March 12, 2018, www.cnbc.com/2018/03/12/some-people-dont-share-salary-information-even-with-their-spouse.html.

5. Working for Yourself

1 "Do I Need to Charge GST/HST?" H&R Block, February 4, 2021, www.hrblock.ca/blog/do-i-need-to-charge-gsthst.

2 Georgia McIntyre, "What Percentage of Small Businesses Fail? (And Other Need-to-Know Stats)," Fundera.com, November 20, 2020, www.fundera.com/blog/what-percentage-of-small-businesses-fail.

6. Self-Worth = Net Worth

1 "Inflation Canada 1980," Inflation.eu, accessed June 17, 2021, www.inflation.eu/en/inflation-rates/canada/historic-inflation/cpi-inflation-canada-1980.aspx.

2 Ruth Saldanha, "Canadian Investors Get a 'Below Average' Fee Experience," Morningstar, September 17, 2019, www.morningstar.ca/ca/news/195738/canadian-investors-get-a-%E2%80%98below-average-fee-experience.aspx.

7. Turn Financial Frowns Upside Down

1 Richard Eisenberg, "What Women Must Do to Ditch Bag Lady Syndrome," *Forbes*, March 6, 2015, www.forbes.com/sites/nextavenue/2015/03/06/what-women-must-do-to-ditch-bag-lady-syndrome.

2 Judy Paradi and Paulette Filion, "Why Women Leave Their Financial Advisors: And How to Prevent It," StrategyMarketing.ca, accessed June 17, 2021, www.strategymarketing.ca/wp-content/uploads/Why-women-leave-their-financial-advisors-and-how-to-prevent-it.pdf.

3 FP Canada, "How to Interview a Financial Planner," Financial Planning for Canadians, accessed June 17, 2021, www.financialplanningforcanadians.ca/financial-planning/questions-to-ask-your-financial-planner.

4 "7 Questions to Ask Before You Invest," Ontario Securities Commission, accessed June 17, 2021, www.getsmarteraboutmoney.ca/invest/investing-basics/making-a-plan/7-questions-to-ask-before-you-invest.

5 "Mortgage Payment Calculator," TD Bank, accessed June 17, 2021, tools.td.com/mortgage-payment-calculator.

8. The Busy Breadwinner

1 Robson Fletcher, "Women Spend 50% More Time Doing Unpaid Work Than Men: Statistics Canada," CBC.ca, June 1, 2017, www.cbc.ca/news/canada/calgary/men-women-housework-unpaid-statistics-canada-1.4141367.

9. Digging Yourself Out of Debt

1 Darlena Cunha, "The Divorce Gap," *Atlantic*, April 28, 2016, www.theatlantic.com/business/archive/2016/04/the-divorce-gap/480333.
2 April Fong, "43% of Canadians Say Financial Stress Is Hurting Their Work Productivity: Study," BNN Bloomberg, September 4, 2019, www.bnnbloomberg.ca/43-of-canadians-say-financial-stress-is-hurting-their-work-productivity-study-1.1310556.
3 Pattie Lovett-Reid, "Low Rates Driving 6 in 10 Canadians to Spend Money They Can't Afford, Poll Says," BNN Bloomberg, January 18, 2021, www.bnnbloomberg.ca/pattie-lovett-reid-low-rates-driving-6-in-10-canadians-to-spend-money-they-can-t-afford-poll-says-1.1549945.
4 Kale Havervold, "The Cost of Filing for Bankruptcy a Second Time in Canada," Loans Canada, accessed June 17, 2021, loanscanada.ca/debt/the-cost-of-filing-for-bankruptcy-a-second-time-in-canada.

10. Big Spending, Big Problems

1 Cathy Preston, "Getting an Inheritance? What to Do So You Don't Blow It All," *Huffington Post*, September 14, 2018, www.huffingtonpost.ca/cathy-preston/inheritance-financial-planning_a_23526484.
2 Jan Willem Lindemans and Dan Ariely, "People Should Spread Out Their Spending—So Why Don't They?" *Scientific American*, March 22, 2016, blogs.scientificamerican.com/mind-guest-blog/people-should-spread-out-their-spending-so-why-don-t-they.
3 Jessy Bains, "Renovation Nation: Canadians Spent $80 billion on Their Homes in 2019," Yahoo! Finance, August 10, 2020, ca.finance.yahoo.com/news/renovation-nation-canadians-spent-80-billion-on-their-homes-in-2019-193852002.html.
4 Ibid.
5 "The Best Home Renovations for the Biggest ROI," RE/MAX, February 12, 2021, blog.remax.ca/best-home-renovations-biggest-roi.

About the Author

Sandra Monaco

Kelley Keehn's second language is money, and her mission is to make Canadians feel good about it. A veteran in the industry, she's spent fifteen years as a personal financial educator and more than a decade as a financial professional, and she's learned that everyone has money problems. That's as true for millionaires as it is for people who spend years trying to pay off their student debt.

As an award-winning, bestselling author of eleven books that cover topics including personal finance, the psychology of money, behavioural economics, women and finance, and avoiding identity fraud, she knows what's in the hearts and minds of Canadians when it comes to their bank accounts.

As a speaker, consultant, and media personality, Kelley used to regularly travel across the country, empowering the financial industry, major corporations, and consumers to make more informed financial decisions. Now, because of the pandemic, she connects with companies, individuals, and media around the globe from her home studio and dreams of seeing Canadians in person again one day soon.

Kelley is the financial authority for *The Marilyn Denis Show*, as well as a regular guest on Global, CBC, and CTV. She was the host of the W Network's *Burn My Mortgage*, a CNBC New York contributor, and a *Globe and Mail* columnist, and has made thousands of international radio and TV appearances over the course of her career.

Kelley is proud to have served as the consumer advocate for FP Canada, as a member of the first National Steering Committee on Financial Literacy, as a member of the Ontario Securities Commission Seniors Expert Advisory Committee, and as a board member of the Canadian Foundation for Economic Education. Today, she proudly serves on the Financial Consumer Agency of Canada's Consumer Protection Advisory Committee and is an affiliate member of the Organisation for Economic Co-operation and Development's International Network on Financial Education.

Visit her online at **KelleyKeehn.com** or on Twitter **@Kelley Keehn** and on Instagram **@KelleyKeehnBiz**.